W9-AML-667

M-Powering Marketing in a Mobile World

M-Powering Marketing in a Mobile World

Syagnik Banerjee
Ruby Roy Dholakia
Nikhilesh Dholakia

BEP BUSINESS EXPERT PRESS

M-Powering Marketing in a Mobile World
Copyright © Business Expert Press, LLC, 2018.

All rights reserved. No part of this publication may be reproduced, stored in a retrieval system, or transmitted in any form or by any means— electronic, mechanical, photocopy, recording, or any other except for brief quotations, not to exceed 250 words, without the prior permission of the publisher.

First published in 2018 by
Business Expert Press, LLC
222 East 46th Street, New York, NY 10017
www.businessexpertpress.com

ISBN-13: 978-1-63157-003-2 (paperback)
ISBN-13: 978-1-63157-004-9 (e-book)

Business Expert Press Digital and Social Media Marketing and Advertising Collection

Collection ISSN: 2333-8822 (print)
Collection ISSN: 2333-8830 (electronic)

Cover and interior design by S4Carlisle Publishing Services Private Ltd., Chennai, India

First edition: 2018

10 9 8 7 6 5 4 3 2 1

Printed in the United States of America.

Abstract

The mobile, device-led integration of online and offline worlds has introduced many uncertainties and opportunities. These have driven businesses, researchers, and policymakers to learn more about this rapidly changing domain. To help businesses compete, survive, and thrive in this transforming environment, it is essential to structure their understanding of the field and provide conceptual frameworks as decision aids. In *M-Powering Marketing in a Mobile World,* we present a concise guide for executives in general, digital marketers, and for interested researchers and policymakers.

We identify key emerging trends, develop frameworks based on critical variables, and draw lessons for marketers. The book illustrates the processes by which mobile devices have transformed economies worldwide, the evolving face of Internet usage, strategies adopted by corporations, their applications in retail, emerging data and metric generation processes, as well as policy issues. It explains how mobile devices have become the market's steppingstone toward an IoT-infused environment, a gateway for artificial intelligence–driven marketing processes and the entry portal for a potentially hyperautomated future of consumption.

Keywords

Big Data, Geoconquesting, Geofencing, Geolocation, IOT, Location Intelligence, Mobile Advertising, Mobile Commerce, Mobile Web, Mobile Economy

Contents

Preface

From the 1980s onward, major technological and social trends have transformed the way consumers and businesses interact among themselves and across market boundaries. These trends have redefined parameters that firms use to serve consumers, as well as the needs consumers experience on a daily basis.

What are these life-defining technological trends? First has been the establishment of the Internet and diffusion of mobile interfaces as ubiquitous platforms for all types of communication, engendering participation from all sections of society. While the United States pioneered in these areas, in many cases, other global regions—particularly, Scandinavia and countries of East Asia—raced ahead to create relevant innovations. It is the first time an electronic channel has reached pervasively into what is called the "bottom of the pyramid"—the poorest of the world, half or more of all global inhabitants—allowing consumers from that segment to participate in conversations with businesses to inform their product development, operations, and service processes. Second, triggered by the seminal 2008 paper by Jeffrey Dean and Sanjay Ghemawat on "MapReduce,"[6] a path has been paved by which the average Java programmer could get large numbers of machines to work together, leading to the open source community's replication of the computation engine, and growth of distributed computing. The continuous data captured by technology interfaces have spawned vast and burgeoning databases. The data residing in these—and increasingly, in data clouds—can be processed efficiently by the new computational methods, enabling businesses to translate consumer interaction into feedback and insights that help transform their operations and offerings on a daily basis. In 2013, a White House report estimated the size of the global Big Data repository to be approximately 4 zettabytes, where 1 zettabyte represents 10^{21} bits of information. The richness and volume of data have enabled data-based offerings and services that allow consumers to make more informed decisions. Third, the above changes have led to the development of more tools and strategies that marketers can avail of to reach customers, as well as more types of data-driven processes that can be used to draw inferences about consumers. Overall, these trends of changed consumer behaviors and marketing practices have led to major public policy concerns, including those of consumer rights to privacy and informed consent.

While this book cannot cover the vast, and continually transforming, fields of mobile services, mobile data, and mobile marketing, it represents a pioneering attempt to put these things together between its covers. Just to clarify, the word "mobile" does not mean just a specific device. It refers to a wider array of devices and sensors that allow consumers, products, and networks to remain connected wirelessly on the move. The book is organized into five chapters. A brief description of each of the chapters follows.

Chapter 1, entitled "The Global Mobile Multiplier Effect," illustrates the far-reaching global nature of mobile lifestyles and strategies. Mobile devices and services are aiding the most affluent segments of the world as well as enabling better lives for the billions of global poor. This chapter also points to the basic building blocks of the mobile ecosystems that are necessary at sector and national levels.

Chapter 2 on "Mobile Strategy" starts out by describing the ongoing transition from the fixed web, accessed on desktop and laptop computers, to the mobile web. With mobile becoming the preferred, and often, the only way to access the web, new mobile tools and advertising formats have emerged. Chapter 2 reviews these, and then, offers approaches to and examples of effective mobile marketing strategies. As the mobile-first and mobile-only worlds continue to evolve, such strategies will also need to adjust and evolve.

One clear consequence of the growth of mobile communications is on shopping methods, especially in countries such as China and India, which have experienced rapid emergence and growth of transactions based on mobile devices. In the United States and other economically advanced nations, e-commerce has been attacking fixed-location brick-and-mortar commerce, and mobile has become a major weapon in these retailing battles. Chapter 3 focuses on "Mobile in Retailing." It profiles various types of mobile-assisted shoppers, in a context such as the United States, and offers a framework for understanding and managing the evolving intersections of mobile technologies and retailing.

As pointed out in the first part of this Preface, because of the global diffusion of mobile technologies, there are growing zettabytes of mobile data. The approaching Internet of Things (IoT) will multiply such databases manifold. Chapter 4, entitled "Transforming Marketing with Mobile Data," starts out by discussing the categories of mobile device-linked data, and some of the ways in which such data is being cross-referenced and cross-pollinated with data from other sources. In particular, Chapter 4 outlines the challenges of the Location Data Synchronization Ecosystems and the complexities of Cross-Device Attribution, that is, who gets credit for what and which type of data? The chapter provides several case examples and approaches to improving marketing strategies via mobile data.

The final chapter of the book, Chapter 5, is on "Mobile and Policy Issues." It is well known that nettlesome privacy as well as security issues have exploded into public consciousness. The chapter reviews the main types of privacy and security issues, especially in a world where mobile usage has become nearly universal. Major regions of the world are adopting varying approaches toward personal data in electronic formats. The chapter focuses, in particular, on the European Union (EU) and China, and also offers examples of privacy and security challenges in other parts of the world. It offers basic and sensible policy guidelines for managing most of the problems of data privacy and security.

At this juncture, the only thing certain about the mobile technologies and markets is the blistering pace of change. This will continue for some years, until technologies become more embedded in objects and bodies. Because of this fast pace of change, the content and examples in a book like this have the possibility of becoming outdated before the reader has a chance to access the main chapters of the book. For this reason, throughout this book, we provide examples, but also conceptual tools—which should cross over into new and emerging technologies. At the end of the book, we provide an Epilogue chapter, where we identify things to watch out for in this continually unfolding future.

We invite the readers to join the conversations on mobile technologies, markets, and services at the social media and research repository sites pertaining to this book and its authors.

Acknowledgments

A book like this is the result of the intersection of the intellectual, professional, and personal life journeys of its authors. Here, we want to acknowledge the key factors and influences that have shaped the journeys of the lead author Syagnik Banerjee (Sy) and his chronologically senior collaborators, Ruby Roy Dholakia (Ruby) and Nikhilesh Dholakia (Nik).

Sy's journey for the research on digital and mobile consumers started with his work experiences in sales, distribution, and vehicle tracking across 12 states of rural India. Observing the discomfort of truck drivers in adopting easy-to-use passively connected GPS transponders over tedious human-intervention-based tracking systems sparked his interest to study user behavior in wireless environments. Having experienced and witnessed logistical inefficiencies, sales losses, product wastage, as well as producer and consumer exploitation by middlemen, it became essential for him to understand the mechanics of rural supply chains in order to comprehend how the deployment of wireless technologies could improve processes, product prices, distribution and the lives of users. Interactions with one of his former B-school professors, Dr. Rajat Kathuria, who was a part of Telecom Regulatory Authority of India, exposed him to telecom ecosystems, revenue sharing practices, and ignited further interest in the industry. His employment with Bharti (Airtel)—India's most innovative mobile service provider—further enhanced his experiences with the data transmitted by mobile sensors, and enabled him to have broader visions of a technology-diffused global future.

This book came about because, at one point in time, Sy's intellectual journey intersected with the intellectual journeys of Ruby and Nik. During his stay at the University of Rhode Island (URI), Sy did his doctoral work with Ruby and also interacted with Nik. The doctoral program at URI ignited Sy's intellectual curiosity as to why mobile behaviors were becoming so central in people's lives. The curiosity translated into discovery and scholarship. Sy's work at URI on "consumer ubiquity" is a pioneering example of putting a strong conceptual bedrock under the rapid flow of mobile telecommunications developments.

Sy then took up a faculty position at the University of Michigan–Flint. Scott Johnson, Dean of the School of Management at University of Michigan–Flint, and fellow faculty colleagues at Flint proved to be tremendously supportive of Sy's pursuit of knowledge in this relatively new area of research. Their support for Sy's promotions and nominations for awards underscored their recognition of the value of this research area and their acknowledgement of its importance and impact. Finally, the strongest pillars of support on this journey came from Sy's family: parents, Dipankar and Tapati Banerjee, brother, Satyaki, and Sy's beloved wife, Shreemoyee. Their constant strength and tolerance through the academic journey fueled Sy's endurance at the most difficult of times.

For Ruby, while there is a long intellectual and personal journey preceding the 1980s, a turning point, from the perspective of this book, happened in the early 1980s. The year 1982 was the time when, because of actions taken by the United States Department of Justice, the so-called divestiture—the break up into multiple entities—of the erstwhile near-monopolistic AT&T Bell System happened. Starting from the mid-1980s, telecom markets—in the United States, and later, globally—became open and competitive, eventually leading to a global state of intensely rivalrous mobile services and devices markets that are discussed in this book. At URI College of Business Administration, with the encouragement of the then-dean Bob Clagett, Ruby established a pioneering research program to study the newly emerging telecom and information technology markets.[1] Nik joined this research program soon, becoming an Associate Director of the research center led by Ruby.

The program at URI produced some of the earliest research contributions on telecom, e-commerce, and mobile markets. Doctoral students at URI, working with Ruby and/or Nik, explored cutting edge topics in these research areas. As URI doctoral alumni, many of these folks have become pioneers in their own rights: David Fortin at the University of Canterbury, New Zealand in the field of interactivity,[2] Nir Kshetri at University of North Carolina at Greensboro in the field of cybersecurity,[3] and Detlev Zwick at York University in Canada in the area of data privacy.[4] Sy Banerjee follows in this illustrious tradition at URI, and is well on the way to becoming a leading figure in the field of mobile marketing strategies.[5] Therefore, as a closing part of this acknowledgment note, the authors thank the entities at URI—the URI College of Business Administration, URI Division and Research and Economic Development, and the URI Foundation—that have supported the research programs on telecom and information technology markets.

SB (Flint, Michigan)
RRD and *ND* (Kingston, Rhode Island)
September 2017

Endnotes

For the full citations, and when relevant, hyperlinks to the references listed in these notes, please go to the References and Bibliography section.

1. A very good source for gaining a retrospective view on the work on information technology markets and consumers at the University of Rhode Island (URI), done by Ruby Roy Dholakia and her associates, is the book *Technology and Consumption* (see Dholakia 2012).

2. The classic article from the work on interactivity done by David Fortin and Ruby Roy Dholakia at URI, published in the *Journal of Business Research*, is Fortin and Dholakia (2005).

3. For a multi-year range of the work by Nir Kshetri on cybersecurity, readers may want to start with his paper written during the URI years (Kshetri and Dholakia 2001) and continue on to the work done by him throughout the first two decades of the twenty-first century (see, for example, Kshetri 2016).

4. Over the years, Detlev Zwick has delved deeply into the cultural aspects of data privacy and data security in the unfolding Internet, Mobile and Internet-of-Things (IoT) era. A good starting point to follow his work is an early paper emerging from his work while he was at URI (see Zwick and Dholakia 2004).

5. Good starting points to engage with the work of Sy Banerjee on mobile markets are some papers emerging from his doctoral work at URI (see Banerjee and Dholakia 2008; Banerjee and Dholakia 2013).

6. See Dean and Ghemawat (2008) in the References and Bibliography section.

CHAPTER 1

The Global Mobile Multiplier Effect

In 2014, the number of mobile phones in the world crossed the number of people on the planet. By 2015, almost 95 out of 100 adults in the world, including people in the poorest nations, had a mobile phone. By 2016, even smartphones were available to 2 billion people. In human history, no other technology has been able to achieve that—ever. The impacts of mobile technologies on our lives are profound, pervasive, and prompt. We need ways to grasp these impacts, so that we can cruise with the trends, rather than be crushed by these changes. From a business perspective, this book offers the conceptual framework and practical ways to act upon, and act with, the evolving mobile technology advantageously. Our aim is to offer a conceptual prism that helps make sense of complex, fast-paced mobile technology settings.

In this chapter, we begin with an overview of the changes that mobile technologies are bringing about all over the world—often in locations that one does not associate with advanced technologies. We next show how mobile technologies act as multipliers—with beneficial ripple effects in the economy and society. We present some ways of systematically understanding the evolution and interactions of mobile technologies.

The Amazing Ever-Morphing M-World

Mobile technology innovations, of course, are occurring, quite expectedly, in the advanced and affluent economies of North America, Europe, and parts of East Asia (especially in Japan, South Korea, Hong Kong, Taiwan, and Singapore). A somewhat surprising aspect of mobile technologies is that innovations are also occurring in developing countries whose vast populations may not have the resources to afford high-end, smart handheld (or wearable) devices or to subscribe to high-bandwidth data plans, but can afford basic mobile access. The big change that has happened is that basic mobile devices (and increasingly, even low-priced Chinese-made smartphones) and simple prepaid plans are now within the reach of even the poor of the planet. As we survey the mobile scene in 2017, here is a sampling of the innovations we observe:

- A mobile messaging app company founded in 2009 with only 55 employees, WhatsApp was acquired by Facebook in 2014 for the staggering sum of $19 billion. What made WhatsApp so valuable was its global footprint, reaching up to and over 90 percent of mobile users in many Asian, European, and Latin American countries. Although WhatsApp was founded in the United States and did its innovations in the United States, it employed an almost stealth approach of building a massive user base outside the United States.
- Watching the success of e-commerce on post-Thanksgiving Cyber Monday in the United States, China launched November 11 (or 11/11) as Singles Day for singles (as well as others) to buy online gifts—for themselves and others. From total sales of $5.14 billion in 2013, the Chinese firm Alibaba generated nearly $18 billion in sales in 2016, and 70 percent of the transactions were done on mobile phones.
- In the field of mobile payments, Kenya's m-pesa has been a trailblazer, facilitating mobile phone-to-phone payments even with basic non-smartphones. Launched in 2007 by Safaricom (a Vodafone subsidiary), it made Kenya the world leader in mobile money systems.[1] Not only do 17 million Kenyans use it, but also 25 percent of the gross national product of Kenya flows through it. One study found that in rural Kenyan households which adopted m-pesa, incomes increased by 5–30 percent. In addition, the availability of a reliable mobile payments platform has spawned a host of start-ups in the Kenyan capital city Nairobi, whose business models build on m-pesa's foundations.[2] Overall, m-pesa has been a true income multiplier for African countries. By 2017, via the resources of global telecom giant Vodafone, m-pesa had entered several countries in Asia and

Europe. In Afghanistan, police officers discovered—to their pleasant surprise—that their salaries were 30 percent more via m-pesa phone payment system than what they were getting in cash, because corrupt officials could not siphon off any part of the electronic payment.

- Text To Change, an Amsterdam-based social enterprise that operates in Africa and South America, set up mobile-based awareness and educational programs through Short Messaging Service (SMS, or texting) for strengthening of school systems, communicating the best available agricultural prices to farmers, providing health care information, and increasing government accountability by making public expenditure data available transparently.

- Blindsquare has tackled the challenge of helping blind people navigate a city with the help of mobile social media. Blindsquare integrates the huge reservoir of crowdsourced Foursquare data with Apple's native Voiceover technology to create a location-based virtual map through sound, to help blind pedestrians find locations on foot or while using public transportation. When the app is enabled, it reads addresses, street names, and surrounding locations aloud. Directions are available on demand.

- Ushahidi from Africa is a crowdsourcing platform built for crisis control, used in several emergencies for mapping location-based insights from text messages, and helping humanitarian groups engaged in rescue operations to pinpoint where and what kind of help is needed. Ushahidi has spread outside Africa also. For example, during the 2010 Haiti earthquake, crowdsourced messages on the Ushahidi platform quickly created interactive maps indicating the locations of maximum damage and where help was urgently needed.

- Abdou Maman Kané, a tech entrepreneur in Niger in Africa, developed an irrigation system powered mainly by solar power, to enable efficient and targeted irrigation of crops. The system can be operated remotely by any mobile phone by communicating with a SIM card installed in the control panel of the pumping and irrigating system.

- In BMW's DriveNow carsharing program, cars use an embedded telematics unit to communicate their position via a Vodafone mobile-to-mobile or M2M SIM card. DriveNow cars are picked up, dropped off, or made available when and where needed. Members locate and reserve the nearest car via their mobile phones, unlocking the car using specially issued Radio Frequency ID or RFID tag.

- BMW's arch-rival Mercedes-Benz has introduced the Car2Go program in Brooklyn, New York, with nearly 500 Smart brand cars, unlockable by the program subscribers using their mobile phones, ready to be driven for short distances at 40 cents-per-minute rental rate, and to be left at any legitimate parking space when done.

The above examples are just a sample of hundreds of mobile innovations occurring every month, in all parts of the globe—advanced nations as well as developing economies. Companies that are relying on mobile technology to build their businesses, especially if they want to be more than niche players, have to reach out to the 4-to-5 billion nonaffluent mobile users in the world. If they do not, they risk the possibility that emerging-economy-based, aggressively priced, competitive companies with vast developing-world user bases may begin to disrupt some of the high-priced, high-margin market segments in Western markets. The hoary truism—"there ain't no brand loyalty that 2-cents-off won't buy off"—holds very true in affluent markets where consumers often have been forced to be in expensive mobile service contracts and plans. There are distinct prospects of mobile innovators, especially from Asia, expanding into Western markets once they saturate their domestic markets. Slogans such as the "The Chinese are coming," "The Mexicans are coming," and "The Kenyans are coming" may turn from improbable jokes into real competitive threats. Even niche players in the affluent world face such threats, though in some strong niches, there may be potential to ward off low-cost competitors for a while. There is also a flip side to this. Personal fortunes and affluence are rising rapidly in many parts of the world, with millions of new middle-class households and thousands of super-rich households being created every month. The rising tide of affluence generates demand for high-end mobile products and services—and this has benefited topline players such as Apple and Samsung. In 2017, for example, tempted by the 300-million-and-growing user base of smartphone users in India, Apple announced plans to open its first iPhone manufacturing plant in that country. Thus, mobile tech revolutions are occurring at both ends—the premium-priced high end and the cut-throat-competitive low end of the market.

Mobile Multipliers: Economic and More

Mobile broadband has both direct and indirect effects on boosting the economy of a nation. Creating mobile telecom networks has direct impact on a country's Gross Domestic Product or GDP via investments in networks, boosting orders from suppliers of equipment (network equipment as well as end-user devices), content and app creation, and more. Indirect effects of mobile telecom include increased productivity, human capital formation (in terms of increasingly skilled workers and entrepreneurs), stepping up Foreign Direct Investment (FDI), as well as portfolio stock market investments as investors worldwide sense opportunities and move investible funds to places where mobile telecommunications are growing. Whether it is farmers using mobile data services to sell their produce to end customers directly, tripling their revenue, or fisherfolk finding the best ports to unload their catches for maximizing the price received, mobile data multiplies productivity of the economy. Mobile connectivity also improves the quality of human capital—directly by making people more skilled in technology use, and indirectly by revolutionizing the state of health and education in developing economies. In some cases, children are learning grammar via SMS (texting) technologies. In other cases, telemedicine is allowing medical care to reach disconnected areas, where image transmission via mobile phones is helping diagnostics.

Figure 1.1 presents a simple schematic model of mobile multiplier effects. The direct effects are clearly visible and easy to trace. The indirect effects are diffused, often contingent on many other factors, but could—under appropriate conditions—be far more pervasive and powerful than the direct effects. The specific multiplier effects, of course, depend on the context. As mentioned, in Kenya and other parts of Africa, for example, multiplier effects of mobile payments are very pronounced, while in China and some East Asian nations, the effects in terms of virtual goods (game weaponry, avatar attires, virtual small gifts) and gaming applications are very noticeable.[3]

Figure 1.1 Schematic view of the mobile multiplier effects

Source: Authors' conceptualization.

States of Mobile Evolution

All over the world, businesses—as well as governments and nongovern-
mental organizations (NGOs)—are on the lookout for ways to extend their
reach and effectiveness via the use of mobile technologies. For any brand,

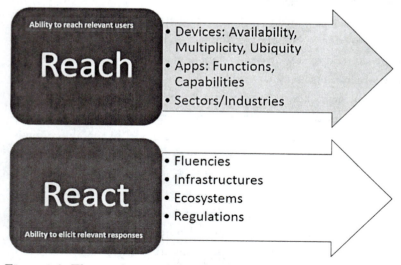

*Figure 1.2 The reach-react framework for effectiveness of mobile
outreach methods*

Source: Authors' conceptualization.

agency, or marketer to initiate campaigns via mobile technologies, it is useful to think in terms of a Reach and React framework (see Figure 1.2).

The Reach dimension encompasses factors that determine how mobile-reliant organizations—companies, government agencies, or NGOs—can effectively reach out to their target constituencies. For example, brand marketers and advertisers may want to reach effectively their intended markets. A child welfare-oriented NGO may want to zero-in on children in need, be they in families or (in strife-ridden settings) in camps or group homes.

The React dimension identifies factors that determine to what extent consumers (or other types of users) can respond to marketing messages (or socially-oriented messages, in case of NGOs). Table 1.1 elaborates on each of the key factors within the overall Reach and React dimensions.

Mobile Technologies and Supply Chains

Mobile technologies are leveling the playing field in terms of tracking and managing long supply chains, for goods as well as services. In the past, large multinational firms such as PepsiCo, Coca-Cola, Unilever, and Procter & Gamble were able to deploy systems to track their supply chains deep into the field. Such firms invested in expensive fleet telematics solutions, which generally included in-cab displays, on-board computers, and satellite communications—the cost per vehicle often exceeding $5,000. Only such giant consumer products multinational companies could justify the cost of such dedicated fleet telematics solutions. Of course, such capabilities continue to be very important for firms where logistics capabilities represent the lifeblood of the organization. For example, UPS has command centers tracking the company's fleets that are often more sophisticated than the advanced command centers of many national militaries, and a mapping system that is far more accurate than Google Maps. By 2017, some UPS trucks were being equipped with drones, for deliveries to remote and off-route locations.

Under the older fleet telematics systems, the small firm with five trucks was left out of the loop. Widely available mobile devices, however, have enhanced shipment visibility across supply chains worldwide, and made the process more affordable for all. With the turnpike fleet optimization device from XRS Corporation (acquired by Omnitracs in 2014), onboard

Table 1.1 Key factors in the reach and react dimensions

Dimensions	Factors	Nature of factor	Description, Elaboration
Reach	Overall smartphone ownership penetration %	Individual	How does it vary by education, income, ethnicity, race, age, etc.? Higher for richer countries.
	Multidevice use	Individual	Number of devices, simultaneous media use. Is attention dedicated, divided, or synchronized? Higher for richer countries.
	Ubiquity of use	Individual	Context of use: Leisure–while waiting, commuting, etc.; Activity–shopping, watching TV, etc.; Social–gatherings, with friends. This influences the physical context and purpose of applications favored by a market.
	Dominant application domains	Individual	Types of functions and applications used most: Native apps, SMS, browse and search, location-based apps. Influences the nature of advertisements and promotions directed at users.
	Industries and sectors with needs	Macro	Are there any particular industries/sectors driving bulk needs for mobile connectivity: Agriculture, fisheries, health, banking, transportation, etc.?
	Nature of sector needs	Macro	Communication, content, delivery systems
React	Technological Fluency	Individual	Aptitude and willingness to use new technologies
	Financial Fluency	Individual	Security perceptions, ability to make personal financial transactions
	Infrastructure	Macro	Network coverage, levels of NFC terminalization,[4] road connectivity for physical delivery
	Development of Ecosystems	Macro	Partnerships among application developers, banks, financial institutions, etc. to facilitate mobile payment gateways
	Regulations	Macro	Extent of government support and friendliness to facilitate fair revenue shares, policy transparency, stability and legal enforcement

Source: Authors' conceptualization.

computer capabilities can be achieved with just $30–$50 a month per vehicle. The size of a deck of playing cards, the onboard device is powered by a cable connector and uses Bluetooth to communicate with handheld devices. For example, an NGO called Food Cowboy uses XRS as well as other mobile technologies to first locate surplus (but still usable and edible) food at wholesalers and restaurants, and then, divert such food away from dumpsters and landfills, to grateful food banks and soup kitchens.

Supply chains of services are also getting transformed through mobile technologies. American health care networks VHA and UHC, the alliance of the nation's leading not-for-profit academic medical centers, merged in 2015. Together, they serve 5,200 health system members and affiliates and provide services to 30 percent of America's hospitals, including the country's Top 10 hospitals. The organization has a mobile strategy and written guidelines on managing mobile devices. Supply chain professionals of hospitals and medical facilities are often on the move at meetings, traveling, or on the hospital floor. Supply chain managers bring smartphones and tablets to work every day to reap the benefits of improved mobility and flexibility. They have discussions regularly with suppliers and distributors and want instant access to information. By providing access to critical price benchmarking data on handheld devices, VHA-UHC prepares medical procurement people for negotiations before they meet or contact suppliers. A hospital in Dallas, for example, may accomplish substantial savings through improved negotiations with equipment vendors in Rochester and Minneapolis by having access to relevant updated pricing, inventory, and competitor information via mobile devices.

Mobile-enabled service supply chains are appearing in the developing world also. In Africa, Kenya Medical Supplies Authority (KEMSA) and Fintech have unveiled the KEMSA's mobile-based commodity tracking application to help in the monitoring, ordering, tracking, and evaluation of drugs for Kenya's Ministries of Medical Services/Public Health-supported health facilities and programs in the country.

Prior to the mobile revolution, tracking and managing supply chains required specialized and expensive equipment, and was engaged in by either large fleet owners, or smaller fleets that carried sensitive or expensive consignments requiring special attention. As a result, developing nations—which primarily had disorganized markets (few major fleet owners)—used to suffer great losses in routine vehicle operations. The wide availability of low-cost mobile solutions, however, has changed the ballgame. Fleet owners with few or many vehicles, carrying sensitive cargo such as diamonds or basic commodities such as harvested vegetables, can now equally afford fleet tracking and planning to improve their respective bottom lines.

Prior to the mobile revolution, remotely tracking and managing supply chains required expensive and specialized devices and systems, or, to use economics terminology, a high degree of asset specificity.[5] As a result, this was a prerogative of an exclusive club of large multinational corporations. With widely available low-cost mobile solutions, the competitive advantages of such asset specificity are disappearing, the doors to the club have been flung open and affordable benefits are available to all agile businesses. Mobile devices and apps are making such specialized assets available widely to all, at very low costs.

The prime example of the world's largest mobile-enabled fleet of vehicles is, of course, Uber, with millions of "free-agent, gig-economy" drivers putting their vehicles in service of the Uber mobile app. Realizing that these cars and Uber drivers represented not just a people transportation method but also a wide-reaching delivery method, Uber launched UberEATS, a food delivery app and system that linked restaurants to food-seeking consumers. By using motorcycles and simple bicycles in addition to cars—in vast urban settings such as Mexico City and London—UberEATS reaches deeper into streets, alleys, and buildings than cars can.[6]

The Mobile Ecosystem

The mobile ecosystem refers to the constellation of the players that exist in the back end to make mobile services a reality. For handheld devices in general, Apple and Samsung have become critical parts of all manners of mobile ecosystems. For network services in the United States, AT&T and Verizon compete fiercely with each other to be parts of mobile ecosystems, and these two leaders face increasing threats from T-Mobile, Vodafone, and others. Specialized mobile ecosystems evolve in specific sectors of the economy. For example, for mobile solutions for trucking fleets, XRS-Omnitracs have entrenched themselves as a core corporate player in the United States.

In general, at the national level, the key mobile ecosystem players are infrastructure actors (equipment makers and network infrastructure owner-operators), basic telecom service providers, content and app developers, value-added service developers, end-use device makers, and others. At the level of a specific mobile application sector, such as mobile payments, the infrastructure has players that are specific to and specialized in that sector. For example, when m-pesa (the mobile payment system that was pioneered in Kenya) entered India, the key ecosystem players included: Vodafone (telecom service provider as well as m-pesa app owner), ICICI Bank (India's largest private bank), Reserve Bank of India (India's central bank that gave regulatory approval for mobile payments), state governments, and local bank branches. The m-pesa mobile payment ecosystem in India, however, is sparse compared to Kenya. In Kenya, m-pesa transactions can be handled by many thousands of retailers and agents, while in India, the regulators require the end transaction (money disbursement) to be via a bank branch—and though Jan Dhan Yojna (JDY) claims to have increased banking access post-demonetization to 99% of households, 21% of chief wage earners do not use these accounts, and there is sufficient criticism about the accuracy and credibility of these figures.

We present two working models of mobile ecosystems—Figure 1.3 is at the national level while Figure 1.4 pertains to the sector level. Technology ecosystems—including those for mobile technologies—consist of a set of interdependent relationships among categories of actors. Some ecosystems are tight, vertical, and smoothly integrated, such as the system from Apple. All the i-prefix and mac-prefix products are owned by Apple, work very well together, and outside service/software/accessory providers must adhere to the exact standards laid down by Apple. By contrast, the Google and Microsoft ecosystems are looser, less integrated, and even relatively open (especially in case of Google). Of course, arguments can be made in favor of the tight as well as the loose ecosystem model—the key is whether users of the ecosystem (developers, end users, service providers, etc.) like it, support it, and want to stay loyal to it, or do they chafe under what they consider arbitrariness and aloofness of the key players of the ecosystem. At more specific levels, mobile ecosystems need to develop their own set of mutually supportive interdependent relationships. In case of the Kenya-based NGO called Ushahidi, the ecosystem includes, among other things, the following: (a) technology

Figure 1.3 Key players in a national mobile telecom ecosystem

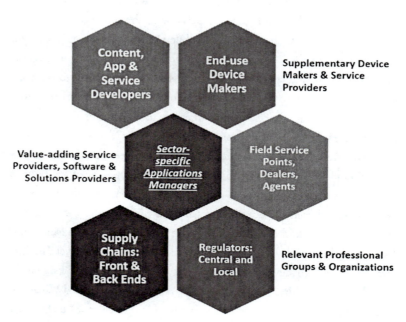

Figure 1.4 Schematic of a generic mobile sector-level ecosystem

tools and platforms (BRCK, iHub, AkiraChix, Gearbox); (b) values and principles (helping the underprivileged, gender equality, community orientation, social justice, promoting democracy, preventing abuses); and (c) future orientations (innovation, entrepreneurship, education, and training).

While public policy and private strategic actions do influence a mobile ecosystem, it is not possible to lay down a prescriptive formula for a good mobile technology ecosystem. Such ecosystems evolve mostly organically, with multiple origins and influences. It is, however, possible to assess the health of a mobile ecosystem. Table 1.2 provides our recommendations to give a "health check-up" to any mobile ecosystem—at the national or sector level.

Table 1.2 System of health check-up for any mobile ecosystem

Ecosystem health dimension	Elaboration, Explanation, Questions	Low . . . . High				
		1	2	3	4	5
Clarity	In this mobile ecosystem, how clear are the visions, values, intentions, and goals of the leading actors?					
Congruence	In this mobile ecosystem, how congruent (pulling together; not working at cross-purposes) are the visions, values, intentions, goals, and actions of the major and minor ecosystem actors?					
Complementarity	In this mobile ecosystem, how complementary (mutually supportive, building on each other) are the actions of the key ecosystem actors?					
Creativity	Taken as a whole system, how creative is this mobile ecosystem compared to other mobile ecosystems?					
Competitiveness	Compared to other mobile ecosystems, how competitive is this mobile ecosystem in terms of attracting venture funding, state support, stock market support, talent, and other resources?					

Source: Authors' research.

The Global Mobile World: Key Trends

Mobile technologies are changing the lives of people, as well as ways of running organizations of all types (public and private), in such dramatic ways that they could eclipse even the technologies of the relatively recent decades—such as TVs and PCs—in a rather short time. The following is a summary of some of the key mobile trends (and of course, this is a continually changing list, which we urge our readers to keep updating):

1. **Mobile Share of Global Internet Traffic:** This share is growing by 150 percent every year. Both Internet and social media access via PCs have declined after 2010.
2. **Rise of the Mobile-Only-Internet-User:** These are populations that do not access the web through laptops, PCs, desktops, or notebooks. The highest percentage of such mobile-internet-only users is in India, Egypt, South Africa, Nigeria, and Ghana.
3. **Mobile Ad Spending:** Ad spending on mobile media increased by a multiple of 5 from 2009 to 2014, from $6 billion to $30 billion. It is estimated to have crossed $100 billion in 2016.
4. **Mobile Payments are growing:** The worldwide mobile payment volume went from $53 billion in 2010 to $163 billion in 2012, an increase of more than threefold in two years. The Gartner group predicts this figure will be $721 billion in 2017.
5. **Emerging patterns of Internet-of-Things (IoT):** Multidevice, Multisensor (wearable gadgets, connected vehicles, homes) connectivity. The Gartner group predicts 25 billion connected objects, including 250 million connected vehicles by 2020.

Concluding Comments

Mobile technologies have become globally ubiquitous—nearly every human being has some access to mobile communication devices and networks. The next stage would entail connecting things—the age of the Internet-of-Things (IOT). The number of connected objects could rise from hundreds to thousands, and even millions, per person. At such scales, the impacts of mobile technologies of tomorrow would completely dwarf the mobile revolution unfolding in the first fifteen years of the twenty-first century. With wearables, vehicles, kitchens, and homes connected—with streaming data, continuous sharing, and barrage of new application programming interfaces (APIs)—there will emerge new ecosystems, players, and revenue sharing practices. To what extent marketers will be able to harness this data to better understand and predict consumer needs will depend on the frameworks we build today to structure the overwhelming flow of data. In the chapters to follow, we provide ways to understand mobile strategies, and comment on how mobile retailing and marketing are transforming with ubiquitous mobile devices and networks. We show the ways in which mobile data can be put to good use by organizations, public and private, and reflect on the significant public policy issues in terms of privacy and security that arise in the emerging Brave New Mobile World.

Notes

1. See Economist (2013).
2. See Weise (2014).
3. For China and virtual goods, see Zhang (2016).
4. NFC stands for "Near Field Communication." It is a chip-based technology. Using smartphones with NFC chips, payments can be made by simple tapping or waving the phone near a terminal that can read data from such chips. NFC is a newer technology and is used in Apple Pay, Google Wallet, Amiibo, and similar mobile smartphone payment systems. NFC chips can be put in credit cards also. Outside USA, especially in Europe, EMV (EuroPay-MasterCard-Visa) chips have been in use in credit cards for a long time. In the United States, the less secure swipe card design of credit cards has led to massive data thefts. It is expected that the more secure NFC-EMV types of payment chips will therefore make rapid headway in the United States—in smartphones and in credit cards.
5. To pursue the concept of asset specificity further, see Riordan and Williamson (1985); and Lonsdale (2001) for a Supply Chain angle on asset specificity.
6. See Filloon (2016).

CHAPTER 2

Mobile Strategy

In this chapter, we lay out the groundwork for using mobile technology tools effectively to enhance marketing strategies. We discuss the strategic use of mobile technology tools in general. We also provide ways to build innovative marketing strategies for a world that is increasingly a "mobile-first" world—a world where users turn to their mobile devices first, for every life activity[1]—and for many leading-edge users, as well as for the majority of populations in the developing nations, a "mobile-only" world.[2]

We begin the chapter by reviewing the role of mobile in the Internet space, its impact on web design and search marketing. We then turn to the challenges of enhancing the mobile presence of a brand, and the tools and apps available (and on the horizon) to do that. While the mobile-first world evolves and grows, most brands have the challenge of building mobile elements in their *existing* marketing strategies (some of which may have evolved over decades or centuries, often starting from the pre-electronic media era). We discuss the challenges of transitioning to the mobile web in the chapter. Next, we turn to the issue of establishing strong brand positioning in a mobile-first and mobile-only world. Mobile technologies provide not merely a means for marketing communications, they also act as marketing channels—for ordering and (in case of digital goods) even for delivery. The final topic of this chapter addresses the ways in which mobile tools can be integrated effectively with multiple other marketing channels, including physical and electronic.

Mobile devices have introduced new tools to compete in the marketplace. Some tools, such as SMS, can be used entirely offline, whereas the rest are online only, or online used in combination with physical context. The following section introduces the changes brought about by mobile internet, designs, tactics, and strategies that work online on the mobile web, and how to apply different tools to reach different types of campaign goals. Within the mobile web section, we start with explaining the transition for marketers from desktop Internet to the mobile era, in terms of the change in audience characteristics and behavior, the evolution of responsive design, and the changes in search marketing strategies.

Transitioning to the Mobile Web

Transition from Desktop to Mobile Internet

In early 2014, the landscape of digital commerce changed forever when Internet usage on mobile devices exceeded desktop-based Internet usage. It became obvious that Internet usage cannot be understood or made sense of without accounting for the device platform it was being used from. With the explosion of multiple mobile devices, the information needs of shoppers went through a process of refraction, causing implications for both website design and keyword advertising. Just like a prism splits an ordinary ray of right into multiple shades of color, the availability of multiple devices separated information needs into two spectral segments—one for situated (desktop) use and another for mobile use. The differences in the two types of needs are accounted for by two key factors, discussed in the subsections that follow.

Users and Devices: Different Users, Different Devices, Different Needs

Within developed markets such as the United States, various studies have reported that mobile Internet users are more likely to be Hispanic, African-American, and Asian, whereas nonmobile users are more likely to be White Caucasian.[3] In the United States, there are both race- and age-based differences. In the developing nations, however, the differences are often related to income: mobile users (i.e., those with total mobile dependency) are often those who cannot afford desktops or laptops. There has been a marked rise in what the media calls the "mobile-only-internet-user" (MOIU), and the profiles of these desktop/mobile users vary, depending on the market. In Egypt and India, 60–70 percent of the internet users are mobile-only, and are mostly below the age of 25. These users shop for different categories of products, use a variety of terminologies to search them, and often use uniquely tailored and culture-specific criteria.

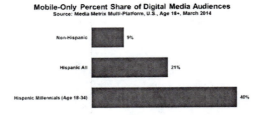

Figure 2.1 *Different users, different platforms: hispanic and non-hispanic*

Overall, then, in any market, there can be: (a) desktop-only or laptop-only situated shoppers, (b) mobile-only-internet-user shoppers, and (c) multidevice shoppers, who use all types of devices and are also known as device-agnostic users. For example, a ComScore study from June 2014 revealed that 40 percent of Hispanic Millennials (age 18–34) in the United States are mobile-only-internet-users (see Figure 2.1).

Users, Devices, Situations: Same User, Different Situations, Different Devices

A person shopping from home on her desktop on a quiet Sunday morning has the time to search different websites, to elaborate her needs and desires, and to compare the available offerings along a range of criteria before making a shopping decision. The same person, on her way to catch a train home from work on a weekday, may use her mobile to shop for products using an Internet smart agent. Under urgency and time deadlines imposed by her physical and life circumstances and restrictions, mobile wins out. This example demonstrates how user information needs vary by the different physical situations the same user is in. The situations, in turn, manifest themselves through different (desktop/mobile) platforms of Internet access.

A variant of the above example is one where the same individual uses different devices to shop for different products. For searching and buying products that require more research—such as a large-screen television, a living room couch, or a car—some users prefer desktops or laptops, because they need to spend more time making their decisions. Such deliberative behaviors are performed more conveniently with a desktop or a laptop. For buying foods such as a pizza or finding new restaurants and entertainment spots, these same users may prefer using mobiles because

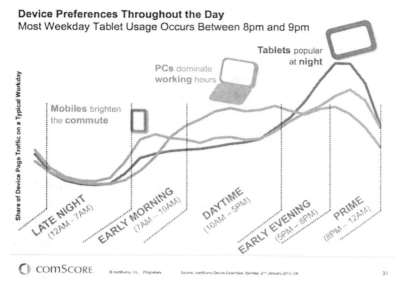

Device Preferences Throughout the Day
Most Weekday Tablet Usage Occurs Between 8pm and 9pm

Figure 2.2 *Device use by time of the day*

the searches and decisions often happen on-the-move. These variations are evident in the ComScore data plotted in Figure 2.2: device use and device preference change throughout the day.

Mobile Design

During the early days of mobile Internet, websites were not equipped to be opened on mobiles. They were desktop-friendly sites. Much of the content of such desktop-friendly sites was not visible due to the layout and screen size of the mobile device. Gradually, there came dedicated mobile websites that required separate links, servers, and maintenance to fit the content on mobile screens. As more and more device models and platforms arrived, it became too difficult to have separate designs and platforms for every new type of instrument. As a result, "responsive design" arrived, which enabled the layout of a particular website to fit devices with any screen size.

Dedicated Smartphone Site

After it became apparent that desktop websites were not suitable to serve the needs of users who accessed the websites on mobile devices, many corporations and brands created dedicated smartphone websites to serve their mobile customers. They often exist as a separate URL (e.g., m.site .com) and are completely different from the full site. They contain features that are considered appropriate for mobile; often, these are just a subset of the desktop sites features.

Responsive Web Design

Responsive web design is a step that goes considerably beyond a dedicated (and usually) limited mobile-only site. Responsive web design is an approach to crafting websites in order to provide an optimal viewing experience across a wide range of devices, with minimum effort directed toward reading and navigation. It has been adopted quite well by mobile marketers. According to the Global Email Marketing Customer Reference Online Survey (2014), 72 percent of enterprise e-mail marketers claim to be using responsive design and 27 percent say they plan to do so. Figure 2.3 provides a visualization of how responsive design adapts the contents of a website across various devices.

Specific or Responsive Designs? Case of Urban Outfitters

Despite the technological and functional benefits responsive design brings to the table, some brands such as Urban Outfitters have been careful about its deployment. They recognized that customers viewing a website on different devices are not merely seeking more of the same—that is, customers are not necessarily device-agnostic. Rather, for a majority of Urban Outfitters

Figure 2.3 How responsive design adapts web content across devices

Source: http://www.celltob.com/web_solution.php

customers, being on different devices are effectively distinct and separable customer experiences, and should be managed in distinct ways. Accordingly, Urban Outfitters deployed technological tools and analytical capabilities, whenever and wherever possible, to make an assessment of what situation-context-location the user was in, and then, directed the user to the website design most compatible with that situation-context-location.[4]

Dedicated Site versus Responsive Design

While dedicated sites make more sense when there is vast mobile traffic, responsive design provides improved accessibility, navigability, and overall functionality to a website, irrespective of the device used to view the site. Responsive design can also save additional costs of hosting and maintenance. Responsive designs tend to retain their functionality in the long term, irrespective of compatibility with new technologies, and hence, are more durable. Responsive designs, however, often add to the weight of the sites (making the sites very data-intensive or "heavy"), thereby reducing the mobile web performance, lowering speeds, increasing bounce rates, and reducing conversion rates. As a result, many brands such as eBay—that need to translate website visitors into paying customers—use dedicated sites. The dedicated sites load faster because mobile customers are very sensitive to website loading speed. Of the top 500 mobile retailers in 2016, 54 percent mobile sites were dedicated smartphone sites, 20 percent had responsive design, and 18 percent had dynamic serving, which is a hybrid of dedicated mobile and responsive design. Figure 2.4,

Figure 2.4 Content prioritization conference—information by screen types

Source: https://www.stunningmesh.com/2012/12/elements-of-a-fantastic-web-design/

for example, shows how Confab, a conference on content prioritization—a challenge that Internet marketers face—varies the conference information by screen types.

Lessons for Marketers about Mobile Web Presence Design

Mobile and situated devices cater to different user needs, based on either different users, or different viewing situations, as explained in our previous sections. Before deployment of Responsive Design, it becomes important for marketers to examine if different users are predominantly accessing the company or brand's website via different devices, if they are using them from different locations and times, and if the website access episodes are being used for different functions (browsing vs. transactions). Accordingly, marketers need to:

A) **Differentiate Content Strategy**: Develop different content of the same website on different platforms. If, for example, teens and kids use the mobile more frequently, the marketer should modify the images, models, and functionalities of the mobile site accordingly—to enable the young audiences to have quick mobile access.

B) **Prioritize Features**: Organize the information with different priorities. Buyers often use the mobile device to navigate to a website when they want to visit a store physically, so links for call-to-action can become more important on mobile devices.

C) **Ad Creative Synchronization**: If the website is ad-sponsored, marketers should ensure that the design of the ad creative elements (images, text, possibly video) are structured flexibly enough to allow reshaping and reorganizing into different shapes and sizes without compromising on effectiveness.

Search Marketing Campaigns: Desktop vs. Mobile

Research and data providing firm eMarketer estimates that the world mobile Internet ad spending will top $30 billion by 2016.[5] This raises serious question about the effectiveness of Internet ad spending. When a major part of Internet access is becoming through mobiles and iPads, how will Click-Through-Rates (CTRs) and Cost-per-Clicks (CPCs) change?

All the data the industry had until recently were results of desktop-driven campaigns viewed by audiences in controlled, private, indoor locations and times (and not the fleeting, on-the-move glances at mobile ads).

In the beginning, some differences were certainly noticeable. For example, Facebook ads showed much higher CTRs on mobile (almost twice) than desktop. Over a period, however, there appeared to be several inconsistencies in such comparisons. Marketers did not know, as outlined in a previous section, whether: (a) the users on different platforms searched different terms, keywords, or spellings for the same products, or (b) if the same user searched different keywords for the same object on different platforms. Some cases would help understand these issues.

A Car Buying Case

A campaign run by the University of Michigan–Flint students for local car companies found that younger users, who were more likely to use mobile for search, are often more flexible, simplistic (use short forms), and impre-cise with word spellings. They mostly used the letters "Corvet" to search for "Corvette," whereas desktop users were more likely to use the correct spelling.

Given that search on desktops is more elaborate and rational, users tend to use more and broader keywords to describe the same object. However, since mobile usage is in more resource-challenged physical situ-ations (e.g., in a rush), the terms and keywords used are more specific. A recent publication by Marketing Science Institute found that mobile tweets were much more emotion-laden than desktop tweets.

The Boy Scouts Case

A campaign run by Heartland Mobile Council in Chicago for the Boy Scouts Association found the following effects on clicks, impressions, and CTRs. Keywords such as "kids games," "activities," and "things to do" were termed as broad keywords, and terms such as "science proj-ects," "summer camp" were considered to be specific. The results found higher clicks and CTRs for mobile in the case of specific keywords, but for broader keywords, the effects were mixed (see Figure 2.5). Another salient observation found that ads clicked on via mobile were at a much

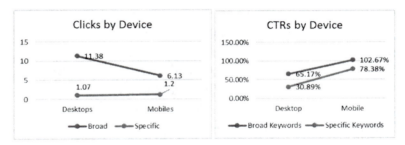

Figure 2.5 *Effects of broad vs. specific keyword strategies across devices*

earlier position (1.46, or near the top of the screen) than on desktops (2.11, somewhat lower down the screen).

How, then, does the effectiveness of these keyword strategies change as we go from desktop to mobile? Here are what current research points to:

- On total number of clicks, broad keywords have a negative effect (decrease) when users move from desktop to mobile, by −46.13 percent. But specific keywords have a slightly positive effect (increase), by +12.15 percent, when users move from desktop to mobile (Figure 2.6).
- On CTRs, broad keywords have a positive effect (increase) when users move from desktop to mobile, by 57.54 percent. But specific keywords have an even stronger positive effect (increase) when users move from desktop to mobile, by 153.74 percent.

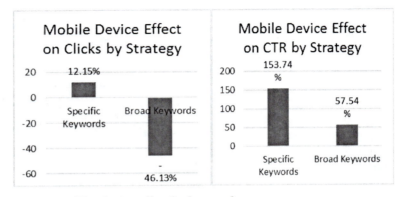

Figure 2.6 *The device effect by keyword strategy*

Another interesting study by SeoClarity of over 2 billion impressions and 2.68 million clicks also found interesting patterns of differences between desktop and mobile CTRs. If the ad ranks on the first position (i.e., at the top of the list of ads), mobiles have a much higher CTR, but that is not true for the second or third position. If the ad ranks fourth, however, it has a higher CTR on mobile than on desktop. So, for reasons that we do not understand fully well, for a mobile ad, it is best to appear at the top (No. 1) position; but, if that is not possible, it may be best for the mobile ad to appear at the No. 4 position (see Figure 2.7).

While mobile user behaviors would continue to evolve, based on the current research on the effectiveness of mobile ads, there are some straightforward implications for mobile marketers:

1. **Differentiated Keyword Strategies for Each Device**: Understand types of customers that use each device, situations when they use each device to search for relevant products, and select keywords accordingly.
2. **Ad Position**: On the mobile, a brand is better off as the top of the second page (or, as a second-best option, the fourth position) than third on the first page. Mobile CTRs are very sensitive to the position of the ad.

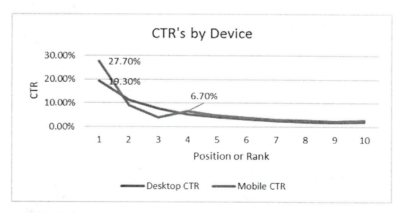

Figure 2.7 SeoClarity study findings on device, ad position, and CTR

Source: https://www.seoclarity.net/mobile-desktop-ctr-study-11302/

Mobile Tools and Advertising Formats

What mobile tools and formats are available and can be used depend on macro factors such as the technology environment, as well as characteristics of the target market. How those tools are used depend on the marketing/campaign goals which, in turn, are dependent on micro factors such as the nature of product/service industry, as well as the needs of the concerned organization. Figure 2.8 lays out a broad strategy framework that mobile marketers can employ.

Understanding the Contexts of Mobile Ads

Technology Environment

Mobile marketing strategies—being reliant on specific devices and tools—require a number of technology platforms, conventions, and standards to work in harmony. For example, brands that want to go beyond merely providing product information and ads via mobile

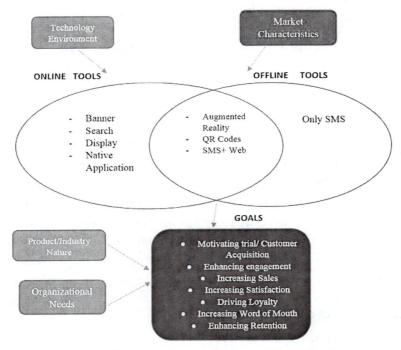

Figure 2.8 A broad strategy framework for mobile marketing

devices will have to engage and facilitate online and in-store transactions. They need to work in tandem with not just mobile operating systems such as Apple's iOS and Android, but also with payment systems such as Apple Pay and Google Wallet, and possibly even more platforms and standards. Table 2.1 portrays the main mobile platforms and conventions available in 2017. Two forces influence these technology platforms—innovations (which could, and likely would, add to—or significantly alter—the list in Table 2.1), and competition (which determines which standards and platforms come out on top). In terms of competition of mobile operating systems and design dominance, for example, in early 2015, a technology blogger offered the following tongue-in-cheek assessment, and a warning that Android better shape up fast or risk becoming obsolete[6]:

> Apple's unified platform and single brand is a formidable combo when Android is fragmented by every measure that matters—number of competing brands, OS [operating system] versions across devices, and varied, inconsistent user experiences because of UIs [user interfaces] like HTC's Sense or Samsung TouchWiz. Androids compete against one another, *and* [against] *Apple* [. . .] while the fruit-logo company [Apple] is a distinct brand standing against the many.

Often, brands—rather than trying to do all their mobile marketing in-house—make the decision to outsource application engagement and Return-on-Investment or ROI (i.e., ways to maximize earnings for a given mobile marketing spend) to specialized mobile marketing platforms. The platforms then deploy messaging, push notifications, A/B Testing (also called split testing, comparing two versions of a website to see which works better), analytics, and a host of other tools to keep customers interested in the brand offerings. Companies such as Leanplum, which tripled their revenues during 2014–16, serve brands such as Tinder, Lyft, Zynga, and Macy's, and track almost 4 billion events a day to function as a dedicated mobile marketing platform. For example, to enhance the push effectiveness of mobile notifications, in May 2017, Leanplum announced a big list of power words, some of which are profiled in Table 2.2.

Table 2.1 Main mobile technology platforms, formats, and standards for marketing purposes

Name	Type	Creator, Owner, Manager	Comments
iOS	Operating System	Apple	Like Windows from Microsoft, iOS is a constantly improving and upgrading operating system for Apple's mobile devices.
Android	Operating System	Google	Multiple flavors and variants create fragmentation in this OS standard. Indeed, Samsung may ditch Android and create its own OS.[7]
QR Code	Camera-readable code	Denso Wave, AIM, ISO	Short for Quick Response code, QR code is a machine-readable matrix array of black and white squares, useful for storing web addresses or other information for reading by the camera on a smartphone. Developed by Japanese firm Denso Wave, these codes are now managed by international organizations.
iBeacon	Bluetooth location system	Apple	Some installed iPhone apps can display special offers and other information when the device is within Bluetooth signal range (30 ft/10 m) of a Beacon signal transmitter.
UPC Barcode	Scanner-readable barcode	United Nations, governments, retail associations	The Universal Product Code (UPC) method of coding is part of the United Nations-sponsored Global Trade Item Number (GTIN) system.
NFC	Embedded Chip	Multiple	Near-Field Communication (NFC) chips that use RFID (Radio Frequency ID) signals. Mobile payment systems are major users of these.
EMV	Embedded Chip	Jointly owned by American Express, Discover, JCB, MasterCard, UnionPay, and Visa	Long used in Europe and elsewhere, the Europay-MasterCard-Visa (EMV) chip is an embedded chip in credit/debit cards that provides additional security. From October 2015, it is required in the U.S. but the adoption has been slow.
Google Wallet and Android Pay	NFC-enabled payment systems	Google	NFC-enabled payment systems for Google Android devices. Google Wallet was the first one. Later, Android Pay started replacing Google Wallet.

(Continued)

Table 2.1 Main mobile technology platforms, formats, and standards for marketing purposes (Continued)

Name	Type	Creator, Owner, Manager	Comments
Apple Pay	NFC-enabled payment systems	Apple	Contactless payment system that uses embedded NFC chips in iPhones and other devices, linked to the user's account, to make payment by waving the device.
Amiibo	Gaming Interface	Nintendo	Interactive toys that can be used with Nintendo consoles and gaming systems.
Apple Passbook and Apple Wallet	Database App	Apple	First called Apple Passbook, then Apple Wallet, and then, simply Wallet, this iPhone (and other device) app stores credit/debit cards, tickets, passes, reward numbers, offers, and more.
Fitbit	Wearable Device	Fitbit	Although designed as a wearable comprehensive physical activity tracker, Fitbit is gradually adding features to make it a full-fledged mobile device.
Smartwatches	Wearable Devices	Multiple	Apple, LG, Samsung are major players. Many established watch brands are introducing connected and networked smart models.

Source: Authors' research.

Table 2.2 Selected power words for mobile push notifications

Power word category	Purpose	Sample power words
Urgency	Impress upon the users that this is time-sensitive notification. And urge them to interact with an app on an urgent basis	*alert, breaking, critical, deadline, reminder*
Exclusivity	Communicate to the users that they are special, and are being rewarded with a unique and special offer	*accepted, eligible, invitation, member, spotlight*
Heightened Emotivism	Words that spark feelings, pique unique interests, connect with the user at a deep emotive level	*believe, dream, indulge, memories, surprise*
Great Value	Letting users think that they are getting really great savings, discounts, or deals	*bargains, buy, cash, deals, offers*

Source: Authors' tabulation based on Leanplum (2017).

Market Characteristics

Psychographic factors such as technology readiness, use innovativeness, and consumer ubiquity; and demographics such as device ownership, education, and income can determine how easily consumers adopt new tools—and which tools are more effective in terms of reaching them. There are also cultural differences that influence, for example, how intrusive push notifications and location tracking are regarded in privacy-sensitive individualistic cultures and multitasking-friendly collectivistic cultures. Sometimes, factors such as English literacy and language skills determine whether mobile audio or visual tools (like augmented reality (AR)) are more effective instead of text-based tools. Internet based tools are difficult to use for mass reach in developing nations as smartphone penetration is low and mobile internet connectivity is prohibitively expensive. In 2016, a United Nations report on the state of global connectivity estimated that approximately 43 percent of the world population used the Internet in 2015, but among LDCs (least developed countries), that percentage was merely 9.5 percent. In 2016, in a country like India, a land of 1.25 billion people, only 200–250 million are online. As a result, in India, when compared to the United States, online tools such as banner ads and search marketing are far more limited in their effectiveness. Firms such as Google and Facebook are acutely aware of this. These companies are attempting to increase the reach of public, free Wi-Fi, as well as low-cost Wi-Fi, in countries like India. In March 2017, for example, Facebook launched ultra-low-cost Express Wi-Fi hotspots in India, with 700 hotspots initially and a plan of rapid scale-up to 20,000 hotspots in a very short time. The usage costs for Express Wi-Fi could be as low as $0.15 per day or $3 per month.[8]

Mobile Tools

Offline

The most common is SMS (Short Messaging Service), which can be used to forward coupons, promotions, and deals. It is a text messaging service component of phone, web, or mobile communication systems. SMS became the primary killer app hat helped penetrate most markets, especially developing markets that lacked sufficient communication infrastructure. SMS is still used in developed markets such as the United Kingdom and the United States for sharing deals, discounts, or important convenience-related information, but SMS use is far greater in the developing nations.

Online

The mobile version of online ad formats such as Banner Ads, and search and display advertising, are also quite popular. According to the IAB/PwC Internet Ad Revenue report 2013, of the nearly $18 billion spent globally on mobile advertising, 38 percent was display advertising, 52 percent was search, and 8–9 percent of the expenditure was on messaging. Pure offline messaging, as can be expected, is on the decline.

Mixed Online and Offline Modes

Both QR Codes and Augmented Reality (AR) applications have supplemented standard offline media such as billboards, posters, and various physical objects, enabling these to transform into interfaces with digital interconnects. This is the domain with most exotic applications, and poised for future growth. Though QR Codes have declined in popularity, AR is all set to take off, popularized by early applications such as Google Glass (which did not quite take off, as expected; but did find factory-floor applications), with Microsoft, Apple, Facebook, and others (including, of course, Google-Alphabet) working hard to bring AR products to market.

Goals for Mobile Marketing Campaigns

We visualize marketing goals in an order of depth of the customer relationship. When customers are new to the brand, it is vital to motivate trial, usage, and engagement—to trigger sales. Once they become regular paying customers, it becomes important to build satisfaction, enhance loyalty, motivate repurchase, and improve customer retention. These goals can be influenced partly by the product category of the brand. Brands that cater to hedonic or sensory-emotional goals try to drive campaigns with more experiential outcomes. In contrast, brands that focus on utility or performance try to deliver rational goals. For example, entertainment houses such as Disney would try to reach more experiential outcomes using AR applications and rich interactive tools. Grocery brands such as Walmart or insurance brands such as Geico, on the contrary, would like to appeal to the smarter side of the consumer using convenient, timely information. In addition, these goals can be influenced by the organizational needs based on the organization's past history of customer interactions. Older organizations with larger customer bases may want to focus on retention, whereas new entrants may want to motivate trials (and to encourage switching behavior, from older brands to the newly introduced brands).

Roles and Examples of Mobile in Marketing Strategy

Mobile technologies are going to shape marketing strategies for the foreseeable several years—in the advanced economies as well as in the developing nations. Every brand marketer, for each of its significant markets, needs to work out, in a clear fashion, the role that mobile methods will play in the brand marketing strategy. Before explaining how different brands can apply mobile tools to achieve their campaign goals, we present a few examples and cases and visualize them on a Product-Customer framework.

Some Examples: Starbucks, Dunkin Donuts

By the end of 2013, over 8 million people were using the Starbucks mobile app. Over 4 million payments a week were being made in Starbucks coffee stores via its mobile wallet. This represented 11 percent of all the payments to Starbucks. By mid-2015, it was estimated that 1 in every 5 payments in Starbucks was being made through its mobile wallet. For a brick-and-mortar retailer, the success of Starbucks in engaging its customers—12 million mobile app users and counting—via *electronic mobile technology* methods is unprecedented.[9] The success of the Starbucks mobile payment app was not lost on competitors—Dunkin Donuts (DD) also introduced a mobile payment app, and by the end of 2014, there were over 10 million downloads of the DD mobile payment app. By 2017, for Starbucks, the number of mobile app users in the United States had crossed 20 million, and the company was expanding the app in major global markets such as China and Japan.

Case: KLM, Amsterdam

Amsterdam-based KLM, one of the leading global airlines, came up with an innovative way to get passengers to use its mobile app to book tickets and manage their reservations. During a 3-week campaign, KLM offered free business-class lounge access to anyone booking a ticket via its mobile app. Not only were lounge-access coupons sent to the qualifying users' mobile phones (to passbook for Apple users, and to Google wallet for Android phone users), the KLM mobile app sent a location-based push notification to users whenever they were in the vicinity of a KLM lounge.[10] They even ran a KLM surprise" campaign, ascertaining location data from customer tweets while waiting for their flights, mining their social media feeds, and delivering gifts physically to suit their occasion for the travel.

Case of Redbox, USA

Even without smartphones and mobile apps, effective mobile marketing strategies can be created. In its "10 Days of Deals" campaign, movie rental company Redbox urged its users—via physical signs on kiosks, SMS messages, Facebook postings, and e-mail—to text "deals" to the number

727272. On each of the ten campaign days, the users received a deal, via return text, offering between 10 cents to $1.50 discount on a movie rental. Since the discount amount was randomly generated, it created a casino-game-like excitement about the promotion. Redbox garnered 200,000 new SMS subscribers via the initial mobile text promotion, and has made similar campaigns a regular part of its marketing strategy.

Unilever KKT Campaign, India

With creative thinking, mobile marketing strategies can be employed even in settings where even rudimentary infrastructure, such as electricity, is lacking or unreliable. In India, consumer goods firm Hindustan Unilever (the Indian subsidiary of the global consumer goods giant Unilever) wanted to reach out to two states in eastern India—characterized by low income and education levels, but with a huge combined population of almost 140 million. In these states, electricity was unavailable or unreliable in many of the villages, and therefore, TV ownership and reach were low. Hindustan Unilever found that while only 28 percent of the target market had access to a TV, 86 percent had a mobile phone. The company launched a dial-in, free, on-demand mobile radio channel called Kan Khajura Tesan or KKT (literally, "the earworm radio station"). KKT offered jokes, music, and the latest Bollywood content—all interspersed with radio ads for Unilever's mass consumer brands. With the handset glued to the user's ear, the KKT name proved amusingly appropriate. By 2015, KKT was estimated to have reached 20 million households—and brands such as Pond's face cream, Close Up toothpaste, and Wheel soap registered major boosts in awareness and sales levels in the two target states.[11]

Putting It All Together: Goals, Tools, and Products/Services

The starting point for injecting mobile methods into a marketing strategy is to ask the questions: "What is the goal? What are we trying to accomplish, in our marketing program, with mobile technology apps and methods?" Ultimately, as a mobile marketing campaign becomes specific

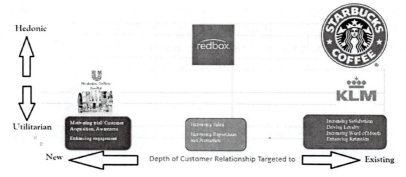

Figure 2.9 Product type, goal, and tool richness

and detailed, the goals have to be expressed clearly in terms of measurable metrics. Initially, looking at Figure 2.9, however, it should be possible to explain the goals in terms of:

- What depth of customer relationship with the firm is the campaign targeted to, and setting the goals about? Are we motivating trials to new customers, increasing sales to some who are aware of the product, or driving higher satisfaction among those who already purchase the products and services?
- What kind of product or service are we trying to promote? Is it a utilitarian product or service, one that serves rational and convenience goals, or a hedonic product that serves sensory or emotional goals?
- How rich (in terms of interaction) a tool does the marketer need to accomplish the above goal? Simpler tools are more affordable, but richer tools are more interactive as well as expensive.

From the case studies plotted in Figure 2.9, we can retrieve a few learning points:

A) Newer customers need more awareness; they primarily seek **information value**. As a result, content is key. In the Hindustan Unilever KKT case, the firm realized that most of the market did not have access to TV, and was starved of stimulating content, which led the company to offer a mobile radio channel to drive awareness. This worked as the company realized most people in that vast, rural, low-income market segment in India were not embedded in a multichannel environment, and there was an opportunity for a new channel to tap into a captive audience.

B) To convert aware consumers into paying customers, smart deals are important to reinforce the *efficiency* as well as *convenience value.* Since Redbox DVD disks were retrieved from physical locations, mobile played an important role in helping interact with the machines. Offering cheaper deals helped more people sign up. In addition, given the different market environment for Redbox, where most customers had access to multiple virtual/online channels, including social media, mobile was used together with Facebook and e-mail to consolidate the effect of the promotion.

C) To drive satisfaction, loyalty, and customer retention, both Starbucks and KLM delivered deeply interactive *experiential value.* One was through a payment app that invited and engaged more interaction. The KLM surprise campaign retrieved social media data based on customer's location (lounge) and activity (waiting for flight) to design and deliver gifts to them.

We can see that as brands target customers deeper inside a relationship with the company, the richer their interaction tools and applications become. This holds for both utilitarian and hedonic products. Once the goals have been set—first in general verbal terms, and later, in terms of specific measurable metrics to be achieved—then the next challenge is to select the mobile technology tools that would be best to reach these goals. One question to ask, based on the above learning points, is this: What kind of value should the brand try to provide the customer to reach this goal? (See Table 2.3).

The possibilities here, of course, depend on the type of goal:

- If the goal is awareness, perhaps it is informational value that the brand needs to provide
- If the goal is to convert into a paying customer, then perhaps the efficiency or purchase value is what the brand needs to provide
- If it is satisfaction for existing customers, the brand needs to reinforce experiential value.

Table 2.3 Examples of mobile marketing goals and effectiveness metrics

Depth of relationship	Marketing goals	Key Performance Indicators (KPIs)	Description
Low (new customer, unaware of offerings)	Retail Application Discovery	App Downloads	Number of downloads of a retail mobile app
		Cost Per Install or Acquisition	This indicates how much it costs to acquire a user (or get him/her to download an application). Usually, Ad Spend divided by number of new installs
		App Store Category Rank	There are 20+ app categories, ranging from lifestyle, business, and education to shopping and social networking
Moderate (aware of offerings, not yet paying customer)	Retail Application Conversion	Account activations	How many have signed up and activated the account
		Items viewed	Which products have been browsed
		Items added to the cart	Products selected for purchase
		Credit Card Additions	Whether credit card information has been added or not
		In-app purchases	Number of financial transactions made within the application
High (paying customers, open to repurchase)	Retail Application Engagement and Retention	Monthly Active Users	Number of users who open the app each month
		Retention Rate	Percentage of users that keep using the app over a period of time
		Average Revenue Per User	Total revenue generated within a period, divided by total number of active users within the period
		User Lifetime Value	Average Revenue Per User, divided by churn (or fraction of users lost in a given period), added to virality or referral value

Source: Authors' research.

In addition, as the value moves from informational to experiential, the tool needs to become more rich and interactive. The simplest mobile marketing tools do not require a smartphone, and rely on SMS or texting. Using these simpler tools, even a small business can drive information value in a number of ways, which are outlined in the next subsections.

Text Marketing (SMS)

Here are some simple mobile marketing steps that even small businesses, including what could be regarded as mom-and-pop operations or even home-based businesses, could potentially take to reach out to, and motivate, present and potential customers:

- Subscribe to a Texting/SMS-based mobile marketing platform (examples of such service companies include Outspoken, mBlox, and Rhombus).
- Select a keyword that represents the business or the brand (say, "FLOWERLOVE" for a Valentine's Day campaign for a florist), and then, motivate users to text this keyword to an easy-to-remember number (such at 575757). See also Table 2.2 for examples of power words.
- To the customers who act, automatically send a welcome message and a thank-you special discount offer.
- Automatically schedule and send future text messages to the responding customers.
- Track the success of such SMS/Text campaign with real-time analytics, such as subscriber counts, sent messages, response rate to coupons, and more.

With smartphones, the mobile marketing campaigns are able to use many more tools and the campaigns can get quite sophisticated. In some cases, of course, existing available tools do not help to achieve the campaign goals, and new tools have to be created. This is what Hindustan Unilever did in India—it created KKT, the new radio music-and-chatter channel, delivered entirely via a simple (non-smart) mobile phone. We will also provide examples of using QR Codes and AR applications.

QR Code Marketing

QR Codes are all about attracting consumer eyeballs to get their attention. This may involve distracting their existing attention to take it elsewhere so as to make the customer aware or informed about a new product, promotion, or experience. In order to execute a QR Code campaign, a concerned brand should identify a target, an origin, a vehicle, a destination, and an outcome.

- Design the content in the *destination*, which is what you would like your consumers to view. It may be a video clip of a new product commercial, or link for taking a survey.
- Decide on a *desired outcome*. It could be a behavior (merely viewing the video), or submitting a completed survey, or visiting a store to respond to an offer.
- Identify the *target consumer*—whether it be a shopper, commuter, or someone else—with specific demographics.
- Identify the *origin*, which is a context highly frequented by the target audience. It can be a virtual context, like a website or a chat forum, or a physical context, which can imply a particular location (street crossing, or neighborhood), time (such as noon, sunset), people groups (friends, festival attendees), and activities (sporting events).
- Once the context is identified, identify a *vehicle* that can easily attract eyeballs within the context and transport attention to the destination for the desired outcome. For a person traveling inside a bus, the vehicle can be the ceiling of the bus; for a person at a party, the vehicle can be a T shirt worn by the bartender; for a commuter waiting at a bus stop, the vehicle could be a billboard, poster, passing truck, or a dust bin.
- Place the *QR Code* on the vehicle so that the target consumer sees the QR code and scans it to reach the destination URL.

Let us look at some examples of the use of QR codes:

1. Emart, the large discount chain in Korea, launched a lunchtime promotion where shoppers could scan a shadow QR code, using the sunlight and shadow only available between 12 and 1 PM. The shadow code gave access to coupons valid only for the hour.

2. To promote the 2012 Europe Cup soccer tournament, Coca-Cola placed QR codes on its containers to connect users with exclusive tournament videos and its SmileWorld social app. This video had a Spanish TV spot on the program—so that people could see the commercial while they were just about to drink from the can.

3. Rockport ran a promotion in Times Square in New York City that featured a giant box with people hanging off the edge. The event launched Rockport's TruWALK line of running shoes. Observers could scan QR codes on the sides of the box to learn more or purchase the shoes.

4. At the Heineken Open-er Music Festival in Poland, attendees were given the opportunity to create their own U-codes, which are QR code stickers that carried personal messages. The codes were a way to help people engage each other and socialize.

5. Procter & Gamble launched PGMobile shopping trucks to patrol New York City, distributing free samples. On the side of each truck, QR codes enabled shoppers to purchase P&G products for home delivery from Walmart.com.

Table 2.4 summarizes these examples of effective mobile marketing, with the use of QR codes. Of course, this is a sampling, and we encourage readers to explore for further examples relevant to them.

Location-Based Marketing

As mobile marketing grows in scope and sophistication, one obvious direction of development is to build mobile marketing campaigns that recognize and take advantage of the relative locations of users, products, retail points, transport methods, and so on. Objects, places, and people—whose location can be tracked—offer opportunities for ever-novel ways of

Table 2.4 Cases of QR code deployment by brands

Brand	Target consumer	Destination content	Desired outcome	Context of origin	Vehicle
Emart	Lunchtime Shoppers	Promotional coupon	Coupon redemption, store visit	Time between 12 and 1	Shadow QR Code Billboard
Coca-Cola	Sports Event attendees drinking Coca-Cola	Tournament Videos, Smileworld social app	Awareness, App downloads	Stadium, event	QR Code on cans
Rockport	Times Square visitors	New Product Commercials Truwalk	Awareness, Purchase	Times Square Event	QR Code on Giant Box with people hanging off the edge
Heineken	Music Festival Attendees	Attendees personal messages	Increase social interaction	Music Festival event	QR Code stickers on attendees faces, T-shirts
P&G	Pedestrians, New York	P&G shopping website	Purchase for home delivery	Streets	QR Code on sides of mobile shopping trucks

Source: Authors' research.

marketing. In this part of the chapter, we review the evolving geolocation strategies of mobile marketing.

Building Georelevance

Proximity-Based Relevance. Businesses need to provide their location-based data to various search engines to be able to come up as relevant options on local search. There are multitude of search engines, and smart agents that collect such listings data. In addition, there are some larger data aggregators such as Infogroup, Neustar Localeze, Acxiom, and Factual, and Foursquare. These data aggregators send information about businesses to local search engines. This way, customers can find the businesses closest to them.

By 2022, the proximity marketing (marketing based on proximal location) industry is projected to reach about $53 billion (MarketsAnd-Markets, 2016). Retail, arts, and entertainment are some of the dominant users, with sports bodies such as Major League Basketball (MLB), National Football League (NFL), National Hockey League (NHL), and National Basketball Association (NBA) using it for event-related promotions. Riding on a variety of technologies including beacons, GPS/geofencing, Wi-Fi, Near Field Communications (NFC), Audio, QR Codes, and LED-based services (review Table 2.1, earlier in this chapter), more than 5 million sensors are deployed globally, a number that is expected to reach 400 million by 2021 (ABI Research, 2016). Approximately 90 percent of the industry is expected to be dominated by beacons (see Table 2.1, earlier in this chapter, the iBeacon row).

Beacon Case of Elle Magazine. A program called Shop Now! coincided nicely with the fall fashion previews that women's clothing-centric magazines unveil in late August. Push notifications were delivered to shoppers in and around the 700 outlets represented by *Elle's* retail brand partners such as Barnes & Nobles, Levi's, Guess, and Vince Camuto. Based on knowledge of consumer demographics and locations inside the stores, push notifications were generated with tailored messages, offers, and shopping suggestions from *Elle* style editors directed at consumers while they were shopping in-store. Overall, the program delivered 500,000 in-store visits and more than 12 percent content engagement for the retailers.

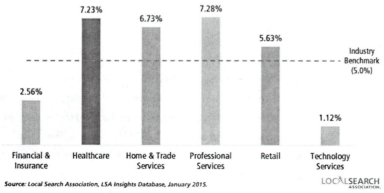

Geo-Targeted Mobile Display Performance
(Secondary Action Rates)

Source: Local Search Association, LSA Insights Database, January 2015.

Figure 2.10 Greater effectiveness of geotargeted ads

Social Relevance.   Foursquare, Gowalla, and Whrrl collect information not only about business locations, phone numbers, and websites, but also connect it to the presence of friends and networks who visit there. Such information aggregation makes some establishments more relevant than others, because individuals know that their friends are there, or that they regularly visit these places. LSA Insights database show that there is approximately a 7-times greater ad effectiveness when using geotargeted mobile display ads.

Geofencing

Geofencing is a feature in a program that uses the GPS (global positioning system) or RFID (radio frequency identification) to define geographical boundaries and effectively design a virtual barrier. This technology helps build the boundaries of who a business wants to target, and it shows increased CTRs. A report by PayPal from 2013 demonstrates that businesses, in general, show increased CTRs when customers are location-targeted, but such increases are the highest in the convenience and gas (petrol) retail categories, where adding location-based targeting increases CTRs by 68 percent. Therefore, as should be evident, some product categories are more responsive to the benefits of proximity-based relevance.

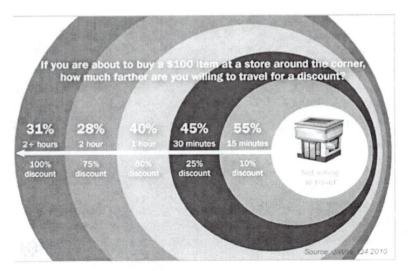

Figure 2.11 Distance-to-discount ratio

Measuring the Distance-to-Discount Ratio.   This metric varies with time, location product categories, and demographic profiles (see Figure 2.11). Companies, therefore, need to study this pattern before designing their geofences. A Ji Wire study suggests that location-based deals can be targeted to users beyond just an immediate vicinity. It shows that 55 percent of customers are willing to drive 15 minutes to get a 10 percent discount, 45 percent can drive 30 minutes for a 25 percent discount, and 31 percent can travel 2 hours or more for a 100 percent discount.

Understanding the Psychology of the Environment

The nature of the location (public/private) makes a big difference to the effectiveness of campaigns. Consumers are more likely to feel intruded by location-based advertisements if they are in private locations than in the company of known/unknown others.

In addition, the task environment can induce negative reactions if location-based advertisements are deployed when consumers are busy at work, causing disruptions in their professional space. Research also shows, however, that disruptions can have a positive effect on redemption of mobile offers in the longer run, if working consumers are not forced to respond immediately with time-bound deadlines.

Targeting User Types

Prior research on the Situated (from desktop at home) versus Ubiquitous (anytime, anywhere) shopper show a few characteristics that help separate shoppers who are more likely to respond to location-based ads (LBAs). From the demographic data profiled in Table 2.5, as of the date of that data (late 2010), we can draw these conclusions about the effectiveness of mobile ads and their appeal:

- Age: younger individuals are more eager to experiment with new technologies such as LBA.
- Gender: Men display more consistent use of LBAs; women's reactions often depends on age, marital status, and presence of children in the home.
- Race: Some studies have found races that are non-White-Caucasian (i.e., African-American, Hispanic, Asian) are more open to mobile (including location-based) ads
- Occupation: Students and corporate workers with tech jobs or managerial jobs are more likely to respond positively.

The Three Levels of Location Targeting

Mobile marketers can employ the following three levels of geolocation-oriented targeting:

- **Geofencing** merely sets a perimeter around a physical location and deploys mobile ads to users within that geographic area. The ad messages may or may not be blended to fit the user's location or include location-based features, such as a store locator. For example, a car service can target ads at only those users who are within half a mile of an airport or train station. Geofencing can deliver a generic message within a specific area.
- **Geo-Aware Ads** detect the real-time location of a mobile user and serve a message modified to suit the context. The message can be adjusted to fit local conditions, season, weather, events, and the like. For example, a coffee shop ad may display directions to

Table 2.5 Demographic differences of location-based service users

Demographics of Location-Based Service (LBS) users		
Demographic	Group	Percent using LBS
Gender	Men	6
	Women	3
Marital Status	Married, Living with Partner	4
	Divorced, Separated, Widowed	3
	Single and Never Married	6
Race	White, Non-Hispanic	3
	Black, Non-Hispanic	5
	Hispanic	10
Age	18–29	8
	30–49	4
	50–64	2
	65+	1
Income	Less than $30,000/yr	3
	$30,000–$49,999/yr	6
	$50,000–$74,999/yr	6
	$75,000 and above	4
Education	Less than High School	5
	High School	3
	Some college	4
	College and above	5

Source: Authors' adaptation of findings from Pew Internet Center's Internet and American Life Project, August 9–September 13, 2010 Tracking Survey.

the store based on the user's location. Campbell soup may send a mobile coupon for a hearty soup on a cold, rainy, dreary day.

- **Geoconquesting** is a variation of geofencing, where a boundary is set around a competitor's location and ads are deployed to mobile users in that area. This method, then, allows a marketer to deliver the ad to customers when they are near a competitor store to entice them to do business with the marketer, rather than with the competitor. Conquesting can also target prior behaviors, and target ads at customers who have visited a certain set of competing businesses in the past. Geoconquesting could be a useful strategy in intensely rivalrous situations (e.g., Pepsi vs. Coke) or in contexts where a new or smaller competitor is trying to attract business away from an established and entrenched competitor.

Case of Outback Steakhouse.   In one of its strategic moves, Outback Steakhouse aimed mobile ads at people within 5 miles of competitor locations. According to xAd, the campaigns performed 80 percent better in CTRs than industry averages. The geoconquesting ads performed equally well as ads served to loyal customers. In post-click activity, however, the more tightly targeted campaigns showed better impact. The geoconquesting campaign drove an 11 percent lift over the general geotargeting in number of people exposed to the ad, who also accessed a store locator on the Outback landing page.

Isolated vs. Integrated Strategy

In some instances, mobile marketing campaigns represent an isolated strategy. In such instances, mobile marketing is employed as the only channel to reach a group of consumers that cannot be reached effectively through any other medium. This also entails a single screen communication campaign—the mobile phone screen is the method of reaching the target consumer. In developing nations, this is often the only or the main mobile marketing option, as we saw in the Hindustan Unilever KKT radio channel case.

An interesting case in the United States is of American Eagle Outfitters (AEO). The company developed a mobile app called aerie. The company sent SMS messages to opted-in consumers who had downloaded the aerie app. They were rewarded with incentives. The SMS messages read, "Whoa! 1,000,000 likes! A million thanks isn't enough . . . be our friend on Facebook." When consumers "Liked" aerie, they received a promotional code for free shipping. The promotion was a great way to build American Eagle Outfitter's social presence.

When mobile marketing methods are used as one of multiple screens—mobile device, internet on a computer, TV, store display screens, and so on—to reach the target consumer, then an *integrated* mobile marketing strategy is in action. Such strategies are increasingly required to reach target consumers who have access to multiple screens and need multiple points of reinforcement. Tusker Beer launched a Team Kenya campaign to strengthen the brand position by aligning itself with Kenyan pride—the comprehensive Tusker Beer campaign included TV, outdoor, print, radio, digital, and in-bar activations. The call-to-action across all channels was via mobile, with the mobile device acting as the unifying channel in the mix. Thus, multiple channels reinforced the role of mobile and helped it synchronize across the other media. These approached are also known as Multi-Screen Ads, where some can be interactive TV ads, some could be promoting mobile apps, as well as some sponsored ads that play along with live TV events.

Pepsi WinView Games Case

Another good mobile marketing example is Pepsi's campaign via WinView Games. Pepsi and WinView Games (a mobile device-based gaming platform) launched the 2016 football season as a free and legal app, available on iOS and Android devices.

Since its launch, thousands of football fans have been playing WinView Games, targeting the 138 million NFL-viewing TV sports fan base, providing a platform for Pepsi to interact with this largely millennial demographic. WinView introduced advertising into the game with the sponsorship revenue being the source of cash prizes for TV viewers who want to play along as they watched live football on TV. The campaign ran through the regular football season, where Pepsi ads appeared live within the WinView app on a weekly basis across five NFL games.

Measuring the Effectiveness of Mobile Marketing

One key aspect of electronic communication technologies that are available for business use and in daily life, and especially of mobile technologies, is the fine-grained traceability of all actions. With devices such as the Fitbit or the Apple Watch, even unconscious actions—such as sleep patterns—can be monitored closely and tracked. Mobile marketing campaigns indeed can be tracked with a great deal of width, depth, and detail.

While mobile marketing effectiveness metrics continue to evolve, the overall categories of mobile effectiveness metrics are essentially based

Table 2.6 *Example of computing different versions of customer lifetime value*

Metric, factor, or dimension	Algebraic symbol or formula	Numerical illustration	Comments
Average customer expenditures per visit (across n visits) = s	n = 100 s = 4	$4	The average customer, across 100 (n) visits spends $4 (s) per visit
Average number of visits per customer per week = c	c = 2	2 visits	The average customer makes 2 (c) visits per week
Average customer value per week = (s x c) = a	s x c = a	$4 x 2 = $8	OK, average visitor spends $8 per week
Average customer lifespan in years = t	t = 20	20 years	Average customer keeps coming for 20 years
Retention rate or percentage of customers who repurchase over a period of time = r	r = 0.75	75%	75% of customers repurchase
Profit margin per customer = p	p = 0.2	20%	Of $100 spent by customer, $20 is profit
Rate of discount (for present value of future cash flows) = i	i = 0.1	10%	Future cash flows discounted by 10%
Average Gross Margin Per Customer per lifespan = Profit margin (p) x Average customer value per week (a) x 52 x t = m	p x a x 52 x t = m	0.2 x 8 x 52 x 20 = $1664	$1,664 is the gross margin per customer lifespan
Simple Customer Life Time Value (LTV) = a x 52 x t	a x 52 x t	$8 x 52 x 20 = $8320	Whoa, Barista . . . average user is worth over $8k
Traditional LTV	= m x (r/ (1+ i – r))	$1664 x (0.75/(1 + 0.1–0.75)) = $3585	Even with future cash flow discounting and erosion of retention, still a big number

Source: Authors' computation.

on the generic categories of electronic communication and commerce metrics. Table 2.3 (presented earlier in the chapter) profiles the major categories of mobile marketing effectiveness goals, along with specific types of Key Performance Indicators (KPIs). The examples presented refer to the effectiveness of a mobile application. Some of the KPIs are measured more intricately than others. While app downloads and items viewed or purchased are easy to understand, cost per acquisition and user lifetime value is richer metrics. Mobile marketing company Fiksu monitors Cost-Per-Loyal-User (CPLU) Index, which measures the cost of gaining a user that opens an app three times. In 2015, that value was above $3, whereas the cost per install was $1.53 for i-O-S and cost per launch was $0.31. Similarly, Table 2.6 presents an example of Starbucks or similar coffee chain computing different versions of their Customer Lifetime Value, developed by the authors from the Kissmetrics Blog.

Mobile Presence and Brand Positioning

A Mobile-First World

Given how large groups of consumers are now "living" on their phones, such a mobile lived reality gives brands a substantial opportunity to position themselves through the device. Unlike other interactive screens (TV/Computer), mobile devices are always in the hand, on the wrist, or otherwise in/on the body.[12] Mobile devices (and the wearables that are beginning to supplement and complement them) are instruments that can be used to transmit customer data to companies to provide valuable insights, and furthermore, these technologies provide customers opportunities to interact with multiple contact points of the brand around whichever location the users and the products/services happen to be in.

Brand Positioning in a Mobile-First World

Brands are reshaping their interfaces and images to cope with the changing environment and changing information needs of consumers. Prioritizing the mobile channel, they are positioning themselves as mobile-first. This is primarily because all around the world, the percentage of MOIUs is on the rise, both across developed and developing nations. As to the question regarding what does mobile-first really constitute, the answer is context. Mobile is different from other electronic devices in terms of its portability, which enables the addition of location-tracking capabilities to marketing and business strategies. Location tracking also allows the device to sense its immediate environment, and enable marketers to build tools that allow consumers to interact with environmental cues; competing and complementary products and brands; competing and supporting businesses; and with people who could be folks known, possibly likeminded, and/or complete strangers—all in their near vicinity.

Two Cases: UrbanDaddy and Walmart App

Here, we present two examples. In the first example, MillerCoors launched the UrbanDaddy Next Move app, which lets Next Move users find somewhere to go, based on who they are with, where they are, and what they want to do (see Figure 2.12). The value of UrbanDaddy (UD) is demonstrated in its ability to record the user's daily and weekly movement patterns to and from business locations and build sophisticated insights so UD can predict their tastes and cravings (such as preference for Kobe-beef Burgers, not just any burgers) as well as choice for apparel and other shopping items.

Figure 2.12 UrbanDaddy app from MillerCoors

Similarly, Walmart has developed apps with which shoppers can identify deals, discover local aisle data, and check in to expedite pick-ups from the counter. Like the UD app, this app demonstrates its value by allowing the users to interact with their environment, and analyze the recorded data for insights. With the main Walmart app, shoppers can scan a product barcode, and then, enter into all manners of in-store and online pathways, to enhance their shopping experience (see Figure 2.13). While the Walmart app serves by enabling and facilitating consumer–store interactions, the UD app positions itself as a smart recommendation engine.

Emergent Examples of Augmented Reality

The mobile-first approach enables interaction with contexts, environments, and locations. AR technologies take capabilities another step forward, by layering and superimposing of information (text and more) on information and images captured of the immediate environment on screen. Here are some examples, and of course, more examples emerge every week:

- Integrated with other Google technologies, Google Glass is an AR application that works with many smartphones and tablets. Google Goggles is a free-to-download Android visual search app. After activating the app, the user enters the camera of the mobile phone or tablet on a building, a painting, a book, a product on a store shelf, or just about anything. Using image recognition and search

Figure 2.13 Walmart shopping app

technologies of Google, the app attempts to present all the relevant information on that object that it can find—historical facts, encyclopedia entries, publishing details, usage instructions, prices (if relevant), related products, reviews, and more. While wearable AR devices such as Google Glass have their advantages in terms of task synchronization, discovery, and crisis response effectiveness, there are also concerns regarding distraction, loss of privacy, and loss of secure valuable information. While the consumer version of Google Glass technology has run into problems, and is generally regarded as a product failure, there are industrial factory-floor versions that are very much in operation, enabling the wearer to see aspects of complex industrial processes that are not visible to the unaided eye. We, the authors of this book, are convinced that Alphabet (parent of Google) would launch one or more AR devices soon, based on the experiences learned from Google Glass.

- The Pokemon Go, an AR game, took the world by storm, for several months. The idea was to overlay digital imagery on a person's view of the real world, using a smartphone screen or a headset. Players traversed the physical world following a digital map, searching for cartoon creatures that surface at random.

- A recent success is SnapChat, which allows individuals or businesses to design a creative announcement or invitation for an event, and upload it at a location and launch a Geofilter based on proximity so that those who log into location services within the specified Geofilter will be able to view the invite and attend the event (see Figure 2.14). Branded Geofilters can cost close to a million dollars, depending on geographic area, date, brand, and reach. The Peanuts movie campaign, using SnapChat and a Geofilter, cost $750,000 for 24 hours for Halloween. Similarly, the Hoopsfix All-Star Classic, an annual event showcasing British basketball talent, employed SnapChat to spread the word about the event across 81,000 square feet. The filter went live the evening before the event and expired just after the event finished. A total of 25 hours coverage was achieved at a cost of $30. By the time the filter expired, it had been used 389 times and received 91,346 views.

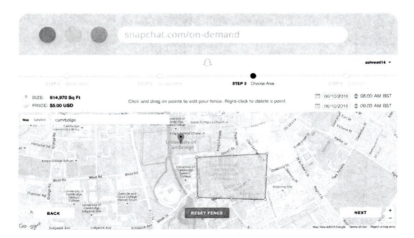

Figure 2.14 SnapChat with geofilter

There are two levels of functioning for AR applications. The first, and the base level is the interaction with the context, acquiring and presenting environmental data, and superimposing the application interface (whether it be graphics or advertisements) for users. The second level is the extent to which user interaction data with the environment can be collected and analyzed. Such intelligent AR can enable sophisticated recommendations, predicting of user preferences, and further allow for multiuser interactions and transactions connected by the immediate environment.

The Future Next: Mobile and the Internet-of-Things

Given the revolution created by increased portability and processing, a future suffused with the Internet of Things (IoT) that consists of billions of smart devices, ranging from digital chips to large electromechanical machines using wireless technology, all communicating with each other, is an exciting prospect. In this hyperconnected world, which is growing exponentially from an estimated two billion devices in 2006 to a forecasted 50 billion by 2020, the system will likely expand to smart homes, cities, cars, health, and fitness among others.[13] Health care fields and health professionals are particularly excited about biometric as well as ambient sensors that could monitor the health and well-being (as well as injuries, accidents, trauma, etc.) on a real-time basis, without requiring a mobile phone emergency call to be placed.

While the IoT technically does not include personal devices such as computers, smartphones, and tablets, these types of devices are often used to manage or communicate with sensors or devices included in the definition of Things. In addition, gathering insights from longitudinal, uneven location-based data will provide a stepping-stone to the modeling and analysis of streaming data emerging from millions of ubiquitous devices.

Concluding Observations

As more intricate data emerge, from mobile user behaviors as well as from mobile location-based sensors, there will be a richer palette of information on real-time environmental variables. This will boost the marketers' understanding of and use of behavioral data. Furthermore, with increasing fields of information to work with, marketers will discover new filters and tools to target their customer bases. New tactics will emerge from the deeper and granular understanding of context that businesses will have access to, including detailed data flows to and from objects embedded in the environments. For marketers, these could be products on store shelves or specific features and prices. With changing strategies and responses will emerge new forms of market intelligence. Even smaller market players, if they are smarter, will have the ability to access such intelligence—regarding their own offerings as well as the offerings of their more powerful competitors. With greater transparency, and greater varieties of tools and strategies to choose from, if appropriate pro-people private and public policies are put in place, then a more competitive environment could emerge that "m-power" consumers. While we, the authors, are marketing professors, our efforts are always going to be (and we urge the readers of this book to do the same) to put the interests of consumers and users first. After all, a world where everyone has to be constantly on the lookout for digital mobile manipulation, rather than benefit from digital mobile enablement, is not in the interest of anyone—except unethical and criminal entities.

Notes

1. A 2015 survey indicated that 71 percent of American smartphone users sleep with their phones on or next to them, with 3 percent sleeping with a phone in their hand. See Ma (2015).

2. For a mobile-only banking example from Brazil, see Boden (2017).

3. See the charts available at Pew Internet Research: https://goo.gl /ZeLZGD. Pew research shows that in 2016, in the United States, mobile dependency was 23 percent for Hispanics, 15 percent for African-Americans, and 9 percent for Whites.

4. See Grennan (2017) for additional details on the Urban Outfitters strategy.

5. By 2021, if eMarketer estimates are reliable, mobile ad spending could top $100 billion. See summary data at: https://goo.gl/cpG1lP.

6. From Wilcox (2015).

7. See Kelly (2014).

8. See Singh (2017) for an account of Facebook's Express Wi-Fi program.

9. Starbucks example based on Halzack (2015).

10. From Moth (2015).

11. From Jarboe (2015).

12. For a deep and psychoanalytic interpretation of mobile devices and the human body, using theories of Lacan, see Reyes, Dholakia and Bonoff (2015).

13. On IoT, see Evans (2011); Kranenberg (2008).

CHAPTER 3

Mobile in Retailing

During the 2014 year-end holiday season in the United States, a number of "showrooming" mobile apps became available. These free mobile show-rooming apps allowed shoppers to compare online and in-store prices for an item, within the retail systems of the same store brand (if the apps were store-branded) or across competing stores if the apps were third-party branded. Inside a store, or even at home, shoppers could scan a product's barcode with the smartphone camera. Some apps had visual image recognition capabilities—even without a barcode scan, based on a photo of the product, the app attempted to recognize the exact product, such as, for example, the title-author-publisher of a book. The showrooming apps then provide instant access to a range of competitors' prices and user reviews, and links for online purchasing.

At first, traditional bricks-and-mortar retailers were mortified that shoppers were in their physical stores, handling and checking out the product and its features, but then using these mobile showrooming apps to scan the product barcodes to do price comparisons. Shoppers then often purchased the items from competing merchants—sometimes online, but at other times, at a different physical location, a competing brick-and-mortar store that offered a lower price for the same item. Later, retailers with a large number of physical stores such as JCPenney and Walmart started developing their own apps that allowed on-and-offline comparisons of product features and prices. These apps attempted to keep shoppers within these retailers' own inventories—in a specific store being visited, at other store locations, and online inventories—and suggesting alternatives to the shoppers if the specific item they sought was not available. ASDA, the British subsidiary of Walmart, went a step further—its

Table 3.1 Selected showrooming mobile apps

App	Creator-owner	Key features	Comments
Amazon Price Checker	Amazon	Via barcode scans, checks prices for an item across Amazon and the merchants on the Amazon website.	Non-Amazon sources are not checked. This could lead to antitrust actions (say) from the European Union (EU) regulators.
Flow	Amazon	Works, for some items (books) via image recognition (no need to scan barcode). With AR feature, Amazon price is virtually superimposed on the item's on-screen image.	Likely model for future similar apps. Also, avoids the sometimes-embarrassing public behavior of "always scanning barcodes".
Google Shopper	Google	Features include barcode scans, image recognition. Also allows voice-based commands.	Often regarded as best price comparison app. Excludes some merchants, especially Amazon. EU regulations could pose problems.
Red Laser	eBay	Mimics the infrared of barcode reader by projecting a (fake) red line on the barcode.	Gives best online prices and, via GPS, the best local merchant prices for item.
Walmart App	Walmart	In addition to scanning and price checking, the app has a "Savings Catcher" feature. Once home, the buyer simply scans the barcode on the receipt. If there are additional savings found, the buyer gets money back.	Merchants with brick-and-mortar as well as online presence are able to offer more features via their apps.
ASDA App	ASDA (Walmart)	Barcode-scanning, recipe-linked shopping suggestions, and more	Extremely popular in UK, and likely to globalize because of the extensive global reach of Walmart

Source: Authors' research.

app, of course, allowed barcode scans, but also provided shopping suggestions based on user-preferred recipes or based on stored shopping lists and past purchases. Indeed, the best brick-and-mortar retail apps are attempting to make in-store physical retailing not only convenient and enjoyable but also compelling—convincing the shopper that online buying is no substitute for browsing the store. In other global contexts, where between 70–90 percent of Internet access is via mobile devices, some retailers are making major, often risky, bets to relying only on mobile apps: in India, in 2015, Myntra—an online fashion retailer that sells over 1,000 fashion brands—dropped its normal PC-oriented website altogether and shifted to a mobile-app only way of selling fashion clothing.[1]

The giant online retailer Amazon benefited considerably from shoppers in competing physical stores doing mobile comparisons and placing orders from Amazon. Ironically, when Amazon started opening its own physical stores, it planned to deploy technological methods to block the smartphones—of shoppers who were inside Amazon physical stores—from accessing competitive e-commerce sites.[2] The 2017 acquisition of the Whole Foods supermarket chain by Amazon raised the possibility that the battle to "geocorral" physical shoppers' smartphones, in this way, could become intense.

Table 3.1 profiles some of the major showrooming apps available in 2015. The strategic intents of the app creators are quite evident in what a particular retail mobile app will or will not do. For example, the apps from Amazon direct the shoppers to the Amazon online store or to retailers who sell through Amazon. Similarly, the eBay app favors retailers on eBay while the JCPenney (JCP) app keeps the shopper within the online-offline JCP ecosystem.

Mobile, Digital, and Retail: How It Is All Coming Together

Retailers—online merchants such as Amazon (which, of course, started becoming multichannel in 2017) and eBay as well as multichannel merchants such as Walmart and Best Buy—have come to realize that the use of mobile phones and mobile apps by shoppers, for finding the appropriate items and for price comparisons, is here to stay.

Physical retailers have also found that their store personnel can be more helpful to physical, in-store shoppers if the store associates are equipped with mobile technologies. In Best Buy stores, for example, associates carry a tablet that can be used for finding items in the store, for price checking and comparisons, and for helping the shopper place an online order if the item is not in the store. Also, in many retail chains, the store associates are equipped with smartphones or tablets that can serve as checkout and payment terminals, obviating the need for shoppers to hunt for a checkout station and standing in line for a cash register to free up. At the Saks OFF 5TH, the discount outlet-style stores of the famous and iconic Saks Fifth Avenue fashion retailer, the store employees, using their mobile devices, are able to check-out in-store patrons. The employee mobile device is able to scan the goods, accept payment, and print a receipt.

Mobile technologies are changing all aspects of retailing, in settings physical and online. By its nature, for most categories, online shopping is more convenient and efficient—and mobile technology innovations will occur faster for online shopping. Brick-and-mortar retailers will have to fight hard, using in-store mobile and other technologies, to keep attracting shoppers into their stores. Innovations that attempt to integrate mobile devices, physical stores, and online shopping are burgeoning. Here is just a sample list of such innovations:

- IKEA has an app through which shoppers scan items and put them in the cart. At check-out, the app generates a QR code that adds up the total amount. The customer can then scan this QR code to pay and complete the transaction.
- Many retailers are developing ship-from-store options, obviating the need for shoppers to lug things.
- On the flip side of this, many customers—after a mobile m-commerce purchase—do not want to wait for delivery, including the express 1- or 2-day delivery options. For such customers, retailers are developing Buy-Online-Pickup-In-Store (BOPUS) options.
- Using the Walmart shopping app, shoppers can simply scan the QR code on their receipts. If there are additional savings on any

of the items bought, the Savings Catcher feature will automatically compute the amount and issue a refund to the shopper's account.

- Again, in the Walmart app, the Search My Store feature does a geo-mapping of the store that the shopper is in, and guides the shopper to the item, obviating the need for a store associate to find an item.
- Stores and malls are adding physical features such as selfie walls and zones, and at the more sophisticated end, virtual reality (VR) and 3-D capabilities that link to the mobile devices of shoppers, to create fantastic experiences that cannot be replicated in home settings.
- Of course, at the cutting edge are drones that could deliver merchandise—to homes, parking lots, and so on.

Categories of Mobile-assisted Shoppers

Retail shoppers visit stores for both utilitarian and hedonic needs. Utilitarian needs are for convenience, savings, and functional benefits—grocery shopping for staple, perishable and or daily-need items represent examples of consumer behavior to meet such utilitarian needs. Hedonic needs are for novelty, variety, and overall experiences that offer substantial

Figure 3.1 Types of mobile-assisted shoppers

Source: Authors' visualization.

emotional and sensory benefits. Going to fancy restaurants, buying flowers for a special occasion, and shopping for a large-screen TV are instances of meeting hedonic needs. The needs of the mobile-assisted shopper are evolving into some distinct segments. Since mobile technologies allow shoppers to interact with brands inside the store as well as allow online access to buy online, in terms of mobile-assisted retailing, the emerging consumer segments are as shown in Figure 3.1.

The segments vary in terms of their mobile in-store engagement as well as their propensity for showrooming, that is, buying products available in-store from an online store at cheaper prices. Table 3.2 profiles the characteristics of these five segments of mobile-assisted retail customers.

Table 3.2 Characteristics of mobile-assisted retail customers

Shopper segment	Description of segment characteristics
Traditionalists	These are traditional physical-store shoppers who prefer to buy inside the store than compare and buy cheaper online. They use mobile devices to text or call loved ones for advice rather than use comparison tools and apps, interactive barcode scanners, or online reviews.
Experience Seekers	These shoppers are particularly motivated by the retail experience, and the opportunity to interact with the store brand on their mobile devices. They are more likely to be influenced by special in-store experiences such as exclusive sales events, preshopping nights, or in-store celebrity appearances. They also exhibit lower price sensitivity.
Price Sensitives	These shoppers are highly motivated by deals, and never purchase products in physical stores if they know they can buy it cheaper online. Unlike the Exploiters, these shoppers do not preplan to engage in showrooming before they come into the store; but may end up showrooming because of cheaper online prices.
Savvys	These shoppers are the most digitally attuned of all. They adopt most mobile-assisted shopping behaviors, including scanning barcodes, searching for a mobile coupon, or paying at checkout via a mobile app. And they are likely to have tablets with cellular data plans.
Exploiters	These shoppers are premeditated showroomers who never purchase a product in a retail store when they know they can buy it online for an equal or lower price. They are more motivated by free shipping, online loyalty rewards, and online return policies.

Source: Authors' research and adaptation from Quint et al. (2013).

In the retail shopping context, mobile-assisted shoppers engage in a variety of behaviors with the help of their phones or tablets. There are three main categories of mobile-assisted behaviors in shopping situations: (a) reinforcing previously planned or intended behaviors (doing what they were planning to do anyway, but with the help of mobile technology), (b) search and discovery behaviors (using mobile technology to find where, and at what price, items sought can be found), and (c) sharing information with others (before, during, or after shopping). Table 3.3 provides further details of these three categories of mobile-assisted shopper behaviors, and indicates the percentage of people engaging in each specific type of behavior.

Retail Offerings for Mobile-assisted and Mobile-synced Shoppers

In essence, the retail industry is seeing the emergence of the hyperrelevant consumer. The emerging hyperrelevant shopper is one who wants all the benefits of physical as well as online shopping, at every location, all at once, in real time. Coined by the network technology firm Cisco and by consulting firm Accenture, the term hyperrelevant customer encompasses the following, especially in mobile-assisted shopping contexts (see also Figure 3.2 for an enhanced and advanced view of the mobile-assisted hyperrelevant shopper)[3]:

Table 3.3 Mobile use behaviors while shopping

Behavior category	Specific behaviors	Percent engaging
Reinforcing Planned Behavior	Maintaining shopping lists	52%
	Using coupons and discounts	45%
	Making a purchase	33%
	Using Loyalty programs	40%
Search and Discovery	Price comparisons	61%
	Finding product information	46%
	Reading reviews and testimonials	37%
	Locating products in-store	21%
Sharing Information with Others	Sharing on social media	43%
	Sharing photographs	49%
	Sharing surveys	19%

Source: Authors' research and adaptation from Quint et al. (2013).

- Efficiency: Mobile-assisted rapid checkout
- Availability: Items be in stock and be easily locatable via mobile devices
- Transactibility: Mobile-assisted ordering and paying, in multiple ways (including storing the customer's preferred payment methods)
- Personalization: In ways that are user-specified and contextually relevant
- Augmentation: Virtual enhancements of physical or digital shopping experience
- Timeliness: Mobile-assisted information/services be available in real time (exactly at the moment needed; not too much ahead of time and not with delays or latencies)
- Ubiquity: Mobile-assisted information/services be available where needed (customer's exact location at any point in time)
- Continuity: Mobile-assisted information/services be available at every stage in the shopping cycle: contemplating, searching, considering, shortlisting, comparison-shopping, ordering, paying, packing, delivery pickup, post-sales service, and so on.

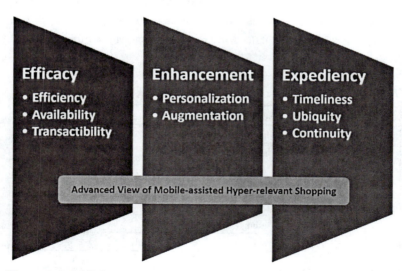

Figure 3.2 Mobile-assisted hyperrelevant shopping: an enhanced and advanced view

Source: Authors' adaptation and enhancement.

With increasing diffusion of location tracking sensors and embedded computing and communicating chips in all manners of objects, the industry is moving toward a broader stage of pervasive communications: the Internet-of-Things (IoT), where information is constantly exchanged in a web among products, manufacturers, advertisers, retailers, shoppers, and more.[4] While the full impacts of the IoT changes will play out over many years, Table 3.4 outlines some of the near term changes that mobile-assisted shoppers seek, and that retailers and brand marketers are attempting to provide.

Hyperrelevance vs. Hypersurveillance

General Electric Company's Lighting unit collaborated with telecommunications firm Qualcomm to develop smart LED light fixtures. These smart light fixtures transmit a code in the light using Visible Light Communication (VLC) technology, and the transmitted code communicates directly with smartphones through the cameras on these phones. The technology can pinpoint exactly where shoppers are in a retail setting. The location tracking is done more accurately than other existing location-based technologies, including GPS, Bluetooth, RFID, or beacon. The location accuracy is narrowed to 5 to 10 centimeters (2 to 4 inches) while other location-finder technologies are accurate only to within a few meters or yards. Using these new LED-based location technologies, on-the-go and real-time special offers can be made to a shopper. For example, while a shopper is trying to decide between Kellogg's Corn Flakes or Cheerios (from General Mills), the shopper's smartphone suddenly might beep with a discount coupon for Cheerios.

This type of pinpoint targeting works especially well for retailers such as discount department stores and grocery stores. In addition to more personalized offers, retailers can also use the customer location data to learn how to display things better and extract consumer insights.

Harnessing the power of location-based technologies, there are many new apps being launched by major retail chains and by independent app designers. Although such apps provide relevant information, and thus, meet many of the requirements of hyperrelevant shopping that we

Table 3.4 *Mobile-assisted shoppers: Expectations and examples*

Mobile-assisted service category	Specific service type	Expectation and elaboration	Current or emerging examples
Product Delivery	Drive-through Lane or Walk-up Counter at Store	Products ordered online be available for pick via a drive-through lane or walk-up counter at the store.	Subway has a remote online ordering and pay option for express service, which has been adopted by almost 27,000 Subway sandwich stores in the USA.
	Same-Day Delivery	Same-day in-home (or at-work) delivery for a small fee	Several companies—including Walmart, Nordstrom, and UPS—are offering same-day delivery, starting at nominal prices (about $5 per order)
	Secure Locker	Pick up online shopping orders from a secure locker at a convenient location	Walmart-owned Asda and South Africa's Makro have placed lockers at secure and accessible locations such as petrol (gas) stations, fast food restaurants—and outside select Makro stores—so that customers can order online and pick up from those locations.
Augmented Reality (AR)	Augmented Offers	Customized special offers and promotions visible when product is scanned using smartphone	Discount coupon distributor Valpak allows customers to download an app where users tap the AR icon and point their phone cameras toward the horizon to see nearby businesses offering Valpak coupon discounts.
	Guidance within Stores	AR apps to guide shopper through aisles and shelves to the exact place where sought item is located	Accenture has developed a new application for Google Glass, which allows customers to explore and discover Toyota showrooms and also check out new car models
	Augmented Content	AR-enabled reviews, in-depth product information, etc. on the mobile device screen	IBM has developed an AR-enabled shopping application that they tested out with UK-based retail chain Tesco. Once the application browser recognizes products on an aisle, it displays information and ranks them, based on a number of attributes such as price and nutritional content
	Visualize Context-Content Fit	Detect suitability of product fit with the need to be placed in certain contexts	IKEA developed an application with which customers can click images of furniture pieces from their product catalogs and superimpose the images

Mobile-enabled Shopping	Smartphone checkout	Scanning of items via smartphone, and paying at checkout also via smartphone	Self-checkout apps such as Stop & Shop and Scandit allow users to check into the store they visit, receive coupons and deals, scan items into a cart, and pay on their app without having to wait in line.
	Virtual Smart Intelligent Carts	Automatic tracking of purchase histories and consumption, via IoT smart appliances (such as refrigerators) to create virtual shopping lists and shopping carts	Cambridge Consultants developed a smart shopping cart that is connected by Bluetooth sensors and powered by wheel movements. Not only does it generate a store map of items on the shopping list, it also transmits location data from the cart to enable location-based deals reach customers as they push the cart to the relevant aisles.
	Smart Payments	Via mobile devices: smartphones, smartwatches and more	Swatch has launched a smartwatch competing with Apple that can make payments from its user interface.
Interactive Digital Signage (IDS)	Checkout Wait Times	Estimated wait times at checkout lines displayed to shoppers	A Lavi Industries study found that Interactive Digital Signage (IDS) at checkout lines occupies customers enough that they perceive wait times to be 35% less than the actual time.
	Customized Offers	Shoppers see offers tailored to their interests and preferences on in-store screens	To help customers expand their palate, Whole Foods aisles of wine, beer, and cheeses use Interactive Digital Signage (IDS) to recommend coffees, wines, and beers to pair with their tastes for dark chocolate or BBQ ribs, as selected by them on screen.
	In-Store Maps	Pointing the location of, and path to, specifically sought items	Ohio-based amusement park Kings Island used IDS to provide way-finding directions to food and attractions, ride features, and specifications.

Source: Authors' compilation from multiple sources, including Accenture (2014), Christie (2015), Vittal (2015).

Table 3.5 Perceptions of mobile-linked information in terms of hyperrelevance and hypersurveillance

In-store use of mobile and Internet-of-Things (IoT) information	Customer perception	Comments
In-store location deals	44% cool	Features are perceived as cool as long as they provide broadly relevant information such as in-store location deals or personally relevant recommendations based on individual interactions. When personally relevant information is retrieved without explicit consent from the user, however, it seems to violate the customers' personal sense of anonymity and privacy—and is perceived as creepy.
Dynamic pricing	42% creepy	
Digital recommendation in dressing rooms	55% creepy	
Salesperson unlocks dressing room	62% creepy	
Facial recognition enables targeted advertising	73% creepy	
Salesperson greets the shopper by name based on mobile trigger	74% creepy	
Facial recognition identifies spending habits to salesperson	75% creepy	

Source: Authors' tabulation based on RichRelevance (2015) and other sources.

have outlined so far, surveys of potential customers also reveal anxieties about the new state of hypersurveillance that such technologies represent. Depending on the context in which the information is provided, the information directed at the shopper can make the application seem intrusive or creepy. A 2015 study by the media and e-marketing consulting firm RichRelevance pointed to major tradeoffs between hyperrelevance and hypersurveillance that shoppers as well as retailers will face, in the near future, as more and more mobile-linked and precise-tracking-capable smart technologies are installed by retailers.[5] In terms of information collected and/or presented via mobile devices, Table 3.5 lists the customer perceptions of "cool" (or hyperrelevant) information and "creepy" information (i.e., information perceived as a form of intrusive, unwarranted hypersurveillance).

Retail and Mobile: A Framework

Depending on their size and physical-vs-online presence, retailers face varying strategic challenges. As retailers' goals move from product trials and sales toward greater shopper satisfaction and superior service quality, they will need to move their mobile applications and tools away from utility and planning, and toward search, discovery, and interaction. Mobile-assisted shopping technologies as well as in-store and online retail technologies have to evolve to keep up with changing technologies (particularly, IoT and wearables), rising customer expectations, and transforming retail settings and shopping contexts. Figure 3.3 is a view of the trajectory that the social-technical evolution of mobile-assisted retailing and shopping is taking.

The different dimensions of service quality reveal that retailers in the first stage would benefit the most by focusing on tangibility, reliability, credibility, and safety. They are dealing with planned shoppers who are prepared with shopping lists, trained aisle browsing, and rely on ad claims and product content mentioned on packages. Such planned shoppers require consistent store layouts—for convenience, reliability, and credibility in product/store offerings—to ensure that they are able to get the items they are seeking.

The second stage that addresses the customers' need for discovery and immersive experiences is both a sensitive and complex one. This is where novel offerings have the potential to be classified as cool, relevant, or creepy, that is, intrusive and panoptic. At this stage, it is important to retrieve explicit consent from customers before the retailer (or brand marketer) recommends personally relevant options, based on stored data. At this stage, customers may have numerous questions that require answers. Customers may have varying reactions to novel experiences and launches. At this stage, retailer-responsiveness is the greatest need of the hour. Customers require access to well-trained store personnel, with deep product

Figure 3.3 Mobile-assisted shopping/retailing: Trajectory of evolution

knowledge and courteous ways of handling queries. Stores also require well-crafted policies of data exchange—policies that keep a balance between being responsive to customers and protecting their privacy.

The third stage is where customers publicly share their experiences with friends and networks. At this stage, it is important for retailers to understand the way people share information and experiences with their friends, as well as people's needs for self-representation.[6] This is where retailers should cultivate empathy, to meet their shopper's goals. This is when it becomes important to gain knowledge of the shopper as not only an individual, but as a member of a network or a community.

Concluding Comments on Mobile and Retail

In the famous Star Wars series of movies, one of the best titles as well as tropes is, of course, the one of The Empire Strikes Back. The metaphorical idea is of the old system, the one being challenged by new-fangled ideas, employing massive resources to strike back at the new challenger. In retailing, in terms of shopping behaviors of people, the empire of brick-and-mortar retailing is not going to go away without a fight. Just as in the Star Wars movies, the same weapons—such as the light sabers—were available to both the old empire and the new challengers, the mobile weaponry in the retail battles is becoming standard and widely available. In the competitive tussles among the old brick-and-mortar retailers, the (not so) new online merchants, and the newer (and yet-to-emerge) AR and VR methods of retailing, mobile technologies (and the successors to mobile technologies) will continue to play important roles. We saw in this chapter that showrooming apps—that often pull people away from physical stores and into online or virtual settings—are being countered by apps such as Shopkick, which encourage frequent store visits and buying, and the Plenti app of American Express that rewards loyalty to a coalition of merchants.

Indeed, the 2017 acquisition of the upscale Whole Foods supermarket chain by the online retail giant Amazon could open up a range of physical as well electronic retail battle spaces that will take many years to unfold. Industry watchers are speculating about multiple impacts, including these[7]:

- Possible other online-physical retail megamergers, in groceries as well as other retail categories such as discount stores and department stores.
- Intensification of the already-on multichannel and omnichannel forms of competition.
- Rapid spread of "order online, pickup at store" options. These are already very prevalent, for many years, in countries such as Japan. The Amazon-Whole Foods acquisition will accelerate this trend rapidly in the United States.
- Intense pressure on supermarket chains (including Walmart superstores) to respond to the multiple ways in which Amazon will launch omnichannel retail initiatives.
- As Amazon begins to use its physical store footprint to provide very quick ways to make merchandise available for pick up, creative and innovative online disruptive firms, such as Blue Apron food delivery service, will be under pressure to provide ways of same-day pick-up of their merchandise.
- Customers will still keep demanding ways of convenient and very quick delivery (without paying premium charges for delivery)—at home, at work, and in their vehicles or transit locations. Hence, innovations in rapid-delivery methods (including drones) will keep on happening.

In comparison to the significant impacts that mobile media are having on retailing and shopping in the United States, some of the global trends in the use of mobile media for retailing and shopping are even more fascinating. In the United States, from about 2005, the Monday following Thanksgiving weekend is called Cyber Monday and it is the single biggest day for e-shopping. In 2015, Cyber Monday sales were estimated to be about $3 billion, and only a small proportion of the transactions were with the use of mobile devices (a proportion that is, of course, rising fast). By contrast, China created an e-shopping day called Singles Day in 2009. This day is on November 11 or 11/11 (the digit 1 referring to singles). From zero in 2009, Singles Day in China in 2015 zoomed up to $14.3 billion, with over 70 percent of the transactions happening over mobile phones, up from 45 percent of mobile-based

Singles Day transactions in 2014.[8] Indeed, for most of the world's population, growing up with mobile devices as their first and often the main electronic medium, transacting with mobile devices is going to be as natural a behavior as walking into a physical store.

The near foreseeable future would witness some interesting and pitched battles, using mobile technologies, between online retailers and those retail chains with large networks of physical stores. The somewhat farther future is not as easy to visualize, but one thing is clear—the distinctions between retailing online and retailing in the physical store will continue to get blurred. This is because the shoppers and consumers increasingly live in a world that is mobile and always connected, inter-actively social and networked, and progressively virtual in terms of the blending of the real and the simulation of the real. Users in such settings want their goods and services conveniently, on demand—and they are not much interested in distinctions such as physical store and online store. Mobile technologies that deliver seamless shopping experiences in a variety of settings would continue to gain in popularity. We foresee that in the not-too-distant future, the retailing distinctions of today—brick-and-mortar stores, click-only online stores, and brick-and-click blended stores—will become quaint categories, terms that held some sway until the early years of the twenty-first century, and then, faded into irrelevance.

Notes

1. See Jain (2015).
2. See Fung (2017).
3. The ideas about technology-aided hyperrelevant retailing and shop-ping are based on Accenture (2014), Christie (2015), Vittal (2015), and other sources; supplemented by research by the authors.
4. For more on Internet of Things (IoT), see Burrus (2014); Newman (2015); Tarantola (2015).
5. See RichRelevance (2015).
6. See Kerrigan and Hart (2016).
7. Based on multiple sources, including Stern (2017), and authors' insights.
8. See Berke (2015); Clover (2015).

CHAPTER 4

Transforming Marketing with Mobile Data

By 2015, leading mobile marketers were already deploying sophisticated marketing strategies, based on collecting mobile data and performing real-time data analytics. These trends accelerated as the second decade of the twenty-first century raced to a close. Here is a sampling of examples of mobile data analytics[1]:

- High-end clothing maker Burberry employed radio frequency identification (RFID) tags to track as well as assist shoppers in its stores to create a richer shopping experience. When a customer picked up a garment and walked by a display screen, the RFID tag would trigger a video on the screen. The video would show details about the materials of the garment and how it was made. If the shopper gave permission, the mobile tracking system would keep track of all the items the shopper showed interest in and examined, and assist the shopper in making selections that fit the shopper's interests, body type, and budget.
- In its drive-thru lane, a fast food company had sensors to monitor the number of cars lined up in the ordering lane. When the line got long, the menu board would be adjusted. To move the line faster, the menu display screen would show only those items that could be served very quickly. When the line was short, the menu board would shift to a full-menu display mode.
- The Spanish city of Barcelona hosts the cutting-edge Mobile World Congress technology show annually. Therefore, the city decided to become a model of how to use mobile data to help residents

and visitors. The city itself is also becoming a center for mobile innovation. Smart parking meters in Barcelona provide real-time updates to drivers on where to park and allow them to pay with their mobile phones. Smart bus stops provide bus riders with real-time updates via touchscreen panels or on their mobile devices. A citywide sensor network informs people about temperature, air quality, noise level, and pedestrian traffic.

While we have covered how to measure marketing effectiveness with different goals, KPIs, and other metrics in Chapter 2, in this chapter, we focus on ways to transform marketing with mobile data. We discuss ways to identify the types of data that can be extracted from mobile devices; types of databases the mobile data can be triangulated with; and the insights, attributions, and applications that mobile data can generate.

The chapter starts with the categories of data that can be generated from mobile devices. Mobile data can vary with device, as well as with time and location of mobile use. Specific platforms such as Foursquare and Twitter also influence the ways in which mobile data can be used. We then provide information on mobile data synchronization, especially when the data is specific to geolocations. We discuss the key ideas of the mobile data synchronization ecosystem. When mobile data can be triangulated with data from other sources (such as demographics, weather conditions, etc.), there are greater possibilities of developing marketing strategies that appeal to customers. We discuss some ways in which insights and applications can be generated from data triangulation. Finally, we discuss some of the cutting-edge issues of digital tracking, attribution, optimization, and the cross-device attribution chasm.

Categories of Data Generated from Mobile Devices

Though the type of data generated varies widely across types of devices used (smartphone versus non-smartphone), and types of applications installed and used (Foursquare, Viper, Visibility), there is a difference between the types of data directly captured by the phone, versus the non-device-based data synchronized with phone-based data, to generate insights for marketing actions. Examples of phone-based and device-derived data may include:

1. Location and Movement Data: User location and movement patterns can be retrieved for active as well as passive usage. There are various methods, including the GPS chips, cell phone antennas and towers, and use of Wi-Fi hotspot locations.
2. Usage: Types of Voice, Text, Data usage.
3. Financial and Transaction Data: Purchases, spending, history, and patterns of financial transaction records, and coupon usage are examples of some variables that can be retrieved from mobiles.
4. Demographic Data: Name, gender, ethnicity, and other variables.
5. Social and Browser Data: Communication patterns and social network analysis of depth and frequency of communication relationships.
6. Communication Content and Sentiment Patterns: Language, tone, sentiment, and mood patterns from SMS, voice, and image communication.
7. Environmental Conditions: Observing signal interference and reflection patterns from water bodies or tall buildings help in drawing inferences and insights regarding civil construction and urbanization. Accelerometers in some smartphones can help determine how fast a person is moving in a car, bus, or while walking.

Device Type and Location of Mobile Use

One of the questions that remains is whether the mobile device is truly used in a mobile manner, across multiple locations. Without that, users will not interact with multiple environments, not realize the value of the device, and deliver limited fields of information to businesses that wish to use that information to understand their needs. A glance at smartphone use outside as well as inside the home is shown in Figure 4.1.

Figure 4.1 indicates that users tend to use mobile devices more than 50 percent of the total time from non-home locations, when they are locating stores, checking prices, or using shopping lists. The rest of the time—when they are purchasing items, using social media to comment, searching items, or reading reviews—they are doing so mostly from home. We can address the former as uses where users synchronize with their environment—the environment is non-home and therefore mobile, and the user is employing a mobile device. The at-home uses of mobile

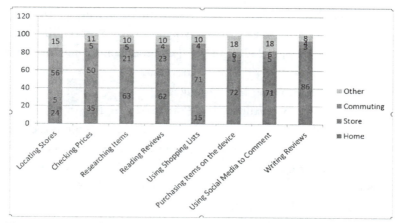

Figure 4.1 Mobile device use: For what purpose? From where?

Source: Chart created by authors from data published by Nielsen.

devices can be characterized as asynchronous uses—the device is mobile, but the user is fixed and immobile. Synchronous uses of mobile devices will generate more environment-related data—in a sense, more relevant mobile data—than asynchronous uses.

Figure 4.2 illustrates how a check-in into Foursquare and a corresponding tweet can inform us about the exact latitude and longitude of the user, type of business establishment being visited, activity engaged in by the user (eating kale), demographics, and date/time—among others.

[In this example, the user—a guy—has an automatic Foursquare Check-In at a restaurant, and then, he generates a Tweet]

Figure 4.2 Application use and location-based social media data

There are further layers in the types of data that can be retrieved:

1. **Direct data:** These are fields of data directly captured and revealed by the phone itself. Examples include personal details, device brand, date-time, and latitude-longitude. Direct data fields can help a company answer simple demographic profiling queries, such as whether men or women are more likely to visit a store.

2. **Synchronized data:** These are fields of data that can be retrieved by matching direct data with other referred databases. For example, name of the restaurant is a synchronized data field, arrived at once the latitude-longitude information is matched against the database of business names and addresses. Synchronized data can be further categorized into static versus dynamic fields.

   a. **Static Synchronized Data** implies referred data fields that do not vary (or are not recorded frequently) across long periods of time. For example, the name of the restaurant is static synchronized data, because the name of the business does not change every hour or day. The name of the restaurant can be further linked to its cultural origin of cuisine. When crossed with cultural dimensional scores of countries, the data can further reveal the extent to which the cultural environment in this restaurant (say, Taiwanese) is likely to be different from that of (say) a French bistro, thereby setting expectations as to how exotic, friendly, or sophisticated the experience can be.

   b. **Dynamic Synchronized Data** implies referred data fields from connected databases that change and are recorded very frequently. This could mean, for instance, the number of persons that checked inside a store; or temperature, or humidity—data that change from hour to hour. This would need latitude-longitude information to be matched against the Foursquare database or geographical weather database. Via sophisticated data analytics, such data can be utilized to tailor special offers. For example, if the temperature recorded and reported is very high, a special discount offer on a cold ice tea or beer can be sent to the mobile devices of users in that location.

The Location Data Synchronization Ecosystem

When location data from a mobile phone is cross-analyzed with data from social media, as well as data from various databases, the potential for generating insights about the marketing context can be enhanced greatly. Let us illustrate with an example (see Figure 4.3 to follow this example).

In this example, we choose location-based social media data that is publicly available to demonstrate how a location-based data synchronization ecosystem works. This ecosystem's primary function is to generate insights and new information updates to benefit existing or new users.

Let us visualize, in this example shown in Figure 4.3, a mobile application that is capable of generating a Happy Atmosphere Index or HAI (higher HAI score implies a better, happier ambience) every time we check into a restaurant. If the happy atmosphere score is calculated based on how many people are at the restaurant, the sentiments embedded in their tweets, how upscale the restaurant is, reviews and ratings left by past customers, hygiene and air quality in the area, then we will use the following entities in building the ecosystem for HAI:

A) We mine the Twitter (social media) API (Application Protocol Interface), which offers public access to its database, by latitude and longitude.
B) We filter the tweets by context, that is, city, neighborhood, and time
C) While storing the filtered tweets in local storage, we connect to four synchronized data sets: (i) The restaurant ratings, reviews, and image

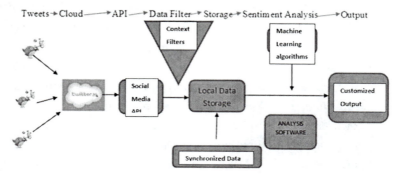

Figure 4.3 Example of a location data synchronization ecosystem

Source: Adapted from Poddar, Banerjee and Sridhar (2017), *Journal of Business Research*

are extracted from the Yelp database for the restaurant, (ii) Hygiene from the public health inspection records database, (iii) Air quality from the smart location database by zip code, (iv) Sentiments are extracted from tweets by the machine-learning algorithm.

D) The software for analysis integrates all the extracted information from the local data storage and calculates the HAI index to create the output.

While the example of Figure 4.3 is illustrative, such developments are already happening in the world around us. Some short case studies on such developments follow.

Nemesis—University of Rochester

Researchers at the University of Rochester developed an alert system called Nemesis. It tracked Twitter posts to flag restaurants where diners were getting sick. The researchers used machine learning and crowdsourcing to analyze 3.8 million tweets from some 94,000 smartphone users during a four-month period. GPS allowed identification of tweets from diners inside restaurants. The processing algorithm tracked those people's tweets for 72 hours, detecting key words related to symptoms of food poisoning, such as "tummy ache," "throw up," "Mylanta," and "Pepto Bismol."

KLM Surprise: Delighting Customers, Generating Viral Publicity

In November 2010, the Netherland-based international airline KLM surprised its customers by having flight attendants greet selected passengers, arriving at security checkpoints and gates, by name and giving them a personalized gift—something that the passenger could use on his or her trip to that passenger's destination. For example, a woman who was going hiking in Rome received a watch that tracks distances and walking speed; a man going to Mexico to build houses for the homeless received a care package of muscle ointment and adhesive bandages; an elderly woman traveling alone was upgraded to first class seating. This gift-giving was a part of KLM Surprise, KLM's effort to connect with its customers on a personal level as well as to encourage social sharing. Flight attendants searched location-based Twitter and Foursquare for people who mentioned that they were taking a KLM flight. Then, using the information the customer volunteered about themselves, the flight attendants purchased a suitable gift and presented it to the passenger upon his/her arrival at the airport. At least 40 KLM customers received such surprise gifts. News of these surprises spread like wildfire through social media mentions, tweets, and retweets, leading to the KLM Twitter feed being viewed more than one million times in November 2010.

Mobile Tracking and Attribution

Illustrative Case of Facebook

How can the mobile data gathering, tracking, measuring, and cross-referencing approaches discussed so far help marketers in improving their revenues? This is where businesses such as Facebook include Mobile Marketing Partners or MMPs, who make measurement and attribution their core business, to improve the effectiveness of the spending on mobile and social media. MMPs connect to thousands of parties across the entire ecosystem, to consolidate mobile data from multiple channels such as push notifications, SMS, email, social media—to properly measure and attribute user acquisition and create advanced targeting/retargeting opportunities across multiple networks. Proper attribution is what allows ad creators to get credit (and pay) for user purchases, clicks, and views. Overall, MMPs have direct access to user-level data via device identifiers. For the MMPs, direct access creates the ability to view and analyze the complete funnel of data, including impressions, clicks, installs, conversion rates, sessions, loyals, costs, revenues, ROI (Return on Investment), ARPU (Average Revenue Per User), and amount of in-app purchases. MMPs are able to report to Facebook on any in-app event, for example, campaigns that may entail installations of apps on user devices. Post-installation, users can complete tutorials, register, and make purchases. Facebook attributes a click to an ad as long as the user had clicked on the ad and installed the app 28 days earlier. Different channels—whether they be referrals, direct, organic search, mobile, or other—are known to play different roles in the process of leading clicks. Some are considered introducers, some influencers, some closers—depending on which stage of the consumer's decision-making they have the most effect (see Figure 4.4).

Media Source	Installs	Sessions	Loyal Users ❶	Loyal users/Installs (avg. 44.25%)	ARPU ❶ (avg. $3,709.42)	NY Business Search (Unique users)
Facebook Ads	9,574	53,084	3,937	41.12%	$2630.33	727
Network 2	3,103	32,874	2,011	64.81%	$3741.87	418
Network 5	4,926	24,419	1,825	37.05%	$2511.39	146
Email	1,759	13,422	957	54.41%	$2743.81	105
Network 4	2,010	8,634	611	30.40%	$2659.33	103
Network 1	728	6,214	388	53.30%	$2809.98	63
SMS	1,211	7,404	549	45.33%	$585.19	69
Network 3	410	4,087	214	52.20%	$3142.07	42
Network 6	380	1,651	127	33.42%	$1070.41	12
QR 1	293	2,896	182	62.12%	$4118.71	7

Figure 4.4 Facebook mobile data ecosystem—one possible illustrative view

Source: Apps Flyer: The Definitive Guide to Measuring Analyzing and Optimizing your Facebook Ad Campaigns

Standard Mobile Attribution Methods

For mobile marketing, and particularly, for mobile advertising to work well, it is crucial to have proper attribution—what devices, actions, and connection led to what effects and outcomes? There are some standard mobile attribution methods in the contemporary world, and of course, more would surely evolve in the future.

Attribution via Device Fingerprinting

One way of mobile attribution is device fingerprinting. In this process, a user's mobile data is collected for identification. This app tracker pulls basic user information—similar to IP (Internet Protocol) address of a computer—from mobile device headers, for connecting dots between conversions. For example, if a person clicks on an ad and immediately goes for an app install, fingerprinting can connect that user behavior. This process works by redirecting prospective customers through measurement URLs, and then, tools gather data from HTTP device headers. The information is then used to generate a unique device-fingerprint ID.

Attribution via Identifier Matching

When an automated app attribution tool matches unique identifiers (whether a customer installs an app or clicks a mobile ad), it is done in real time, saving marketers time and effort. Automated tools support many unique user identifier matches, including app-to-app, web-to-app, iOS, Android, and others.

Figure 4.4 demonstrates an example where the effectiveness of each type of ad campaign was measured, based on attribution by identifier matching, that is, customers' subsequent sessions were identified by matching the installations on their device, which also allowed identifying loyal users and their behavior.

Attribution via Location Tracking

With increasing ability to locate and track the exact latitude-longitude of a user, geo-defined customer targeting offers marketers a way to fill in gaps created by traditional desktop-oriented targeting. Location-based ad targeting broadly entails geo-aware ad placement via a wide variety of technologies. These include beacons, GPS/geofencing, Wi-Fi, NFC, Audio, QR Codes, and LED-based services. Big Data analytic methods leverage such consumer information to detect location, tracking a user's spatial behavior after ad exposure. Measuring large samples of mobile users, via first- or third-party entities, generates behavior patterns (for several segments of users), and thus, sheds light on the entire purchasing journeys (of specific market segments).

The application Foursquare allows for searching places, which can be used to generate recommendations. It has been observed that recommendations—derived from broad Foursquare searches—trigger check-ins to the recommended places, within three days. This implies that search queries and recommendations can be attributed to store visits. Similarly, campaigns can be attributed to store visits as well. There are multiple ways to find out backgrounds of store visitors. These ways include tracking of apps installed and used, background tracking, check-ins, beacon technology, or even surveys. The mobile research and analytic firm YP Marketing uses information of 150 million profiles of users and GPS data, gathered from mobile marketing campaigns directed to store visitors. The store-visit background profile data (see Figure 4.5) are compared to the profiles targeted, analyzed in terms of whether they received ad impressions, and whether the users clicked on the viewed advertisement. A good example is Foursquare's new product, called Attribution. This uses Foursquare's first-party data to measure and determine

Measuring Store Visits: How it works

Compare each visitor to our campaign data:
- Were they in our **profile target**?
- If so, did they receive an ad **impression**?
- And if so, did they **click** on the ad?

10x

3x   0.50%

0.05%   0.15%

Control   **Impression**   **Imp/Click**

yp marketing solutions

Figure 4.5 Matching store visits to campaign data

incremental lift in store visits. We provide more details on Foursquare's predictions later in this chapter, in the section on location intelligence.

While marketers have developed some certainty over comprehending the mobile attribution process—as long as users stay on the same device—with unique identifiers and device fingerprinting, the process is far from perfect. Open URLs (web addresses) with click IDs, as well as cross-device usage and clicks, make the attribution process far more difficult.

The Cross-Device Attribution Chasm

The value of cookies (small files stored on a user's device, readable by the company that placed the file on the user's device) tracking users diminishes as users switch to multiple screens. Businesses are waking up to the new reality of multiscreen, multidevice, multiapp users—often in near-simultaneous ways. Businesses are beginning to grasp the importance of developing a holistic view of consumers across multiple devices.

Currently, the process used is deterministic attribution. When a user logs into his or her accounts across mobile phone, tablet, and desktop, the current ways of attribution create an accurate picture of that individual user, as s/he floats seamlessly across devices. This, however, is a restricted condition. If a user is logged in across devices, advertisers and publishers can use this type of unique identifier to target users on multiscreens with near-perfect accuracy. But for this tactic to be effective, it requires scale—the Big Data ability to capture and analyze millions of data points, in real time. This is likely to work for giant firms that have large user bases and maintain mobile and desktop information that require logins. Smaller firms are less able to do such tracking. Furthermore, privacy red flags go up when any single company—no matter how user-friendly that company's demeanor—is perceived as owning and controlling an accurate map of every device with some level of visibility into every action on those devices. In the Brave New World of mobile marketing—based on sophisticated capturing of multiple data streams and Big Data analytics, and the emerging Internet-of-Things (IoT)—there are going to be several major tradeoffs among the issues of privacy, security, convenience, trust, and fairness.

The other method, the alternative to deterministic attribution, is statistical identification or probabilistic matching. Statistical identification is a technology that captures a range of nonpersonally identifiable device data points such as Apple's IDFA (Identifier for Advertising) and Google's AndroidID. Such nonpersonally identifiable device data—along with rich location, environmental, and behavioral data—can be used to feed algorithms that graph the probability of a user being connected to device 1, 2, and/or 3. This can include device, browser, app, and operating system data—such as checking for multiple devices using the same home Wi-Fi router that are turned on around the same time every evening. This form of tracking is, of course, purely probabilistic (and not deterministic). Some tech firms are also attempting to use hybrid models—deterministic + probabilistic—for identification of the user, device, location, exact use, and more. In all cases, the complex tradeoffs and policy issues that we have alluded to remain open for discussion and debate, in varying forms and degrees.

Predicting and Optimizing Offline Campaigns with Location Intelligence

In September 2015, Foursquare, the location-based app, combined foot traffic data from Apple stores with public Apple sales data to accurately predict that the new iPhone model would sell between 13 and 15 million units during the first weekend. Further, in 2016, they predicted that Chipotle—based on media reports of E.coli infection, raising concerns about the safety and hygiene of their foods and processes—would experience reduced same-store foot traffic by 23 percent and face same-store sales drops of 30 percent. The actual sales fell by 29.7 percent (see Figures 4.6 and 4.7). In this prediction, footfall data from location intelligence—following media reports and coupon promotions—were taken into account.

Using the large dataset of 85 million users, Foursquare executives were also able to suggest that 20 percent of the customers were frequent customers

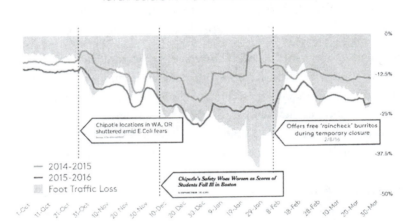

Figure 4.6 Chipotle same-store traffic decline over time

Source: http://www.businessinsider.com/foursquare-data-predicted-chipotle-results-2016-4?r=UK&IR=T

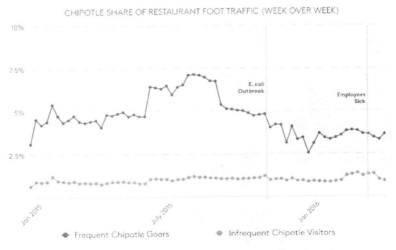

Figure 4.7 Chipotle share of foot traffic over time by visitor type

Source: https://medium.com/foursquare-direct/foursquare-predicts-chipotle-s-q1-sales-down-nearly-30-foot-traffic-reveals-the-start-of-a-mixed-78515b2389af

(i.e., heavy users, to use familiar marketing terminology) that made up 50 percent of the foot traffic visits. These frequent customers, however, as a result of the poor publicity, were more likely to drop off and 25 percent less likely to return. It was the infrequent customers, then, that played a greater role in Chipotle's recovery after the E.coli incidents (Figure 4.7).

Retail Site Selection and Performance Monitoring with Location Intelligence

By using location intelligence, it is easier to measure the potential of a retail trade area. This is accomplished by examining data related to: (a) Locations of existing stores, competing stores, (b) Lot sizes and zoning, (c) Traffic patterns and density, (d) Parking availability, (e) Proximity to third-party operations, (f) Demographics, and (g) Walk times and drive times from different zones within the region. Similarly, based on KPIs, a store is able to: (i) Target potential customers with appropriate sales and marketing actions, (ii) Monitor sales to better estimate market penetration, and (iii) Visualize customer's total value, including high potential of buyers, population density, homeowners, and household income.

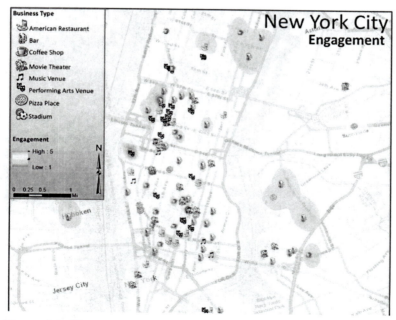

Figure 4.8 User engagement with physical surroundings

Similarly, further data layers—extracted from social media posts made from selected geographical locations—can be added to the picture. See, for example, the map in Figure 4.8. It shows how engaged the users—who are checked-in (via Foursquare) at different businesses in Manhattan—are, with their immediate physical surroundings, at a given point of time. Inside Manhattan, the blue or low-engagement zones are more inward and inland, whereas the yellow or high-engagement zones are closer to the water.

The Value of Mobile Data

Overall, we observe that mobile data holds two broad areas of value. The first is personalizability value. This is when mobile data enables identifying users, connecting channel exposures, demographics, user characteristics, and user reactions via device identifiers. In this way, longitudinal data—spread over a length of time—can be accrued for and associated with users.

The patterns of behavior across locations and times can reveal use preferences, purchase and post-purchase pathways, and use contexts. These can help build more effective user interfaces for applications and businesses, with customized interactive designs.

The second type of value of mobile data is synchronicity value. Although, in terms of neoclassical economic theory, markets are supposed to reach equilibrium when demand and supply intersect, in most cases in the real world, information asymmetry can lead to suboptimal choices for buyers and sellers. With GPS coordinates in mobile data, synchronizing with static and dynamic datasets in the region can remove much of the information asymmetry in real-time interactions. For example, negotiations with taxicabs, cars, and drivers in apps such as Uber are more efficient when consumers know what alternatives/choices they have in the nearby region, synchronizing their own regional location data with that of other taxicab or app-hired-car locations (see Figure 4.9). Synchronicity value is more than mere location data; it is value utilized from the web of variables that can be accessed via the location data.

Both the personalizability and synchronicity values come together with programmatic advertising, in the form of IDFAs (iOS) and Advertising IDs for Androids, allowing for the tracking of the device and user characteristics. An example is the British mobile operator O2's tariff refresh TV ad, which was made relevant and engaging for a mobile audience.

Figure 4.9 Synchronicity value-cabs in the area

A system was designed to take data about mobile usage—device, location, and more—and then, create and offer users specific messages based on that profile. O2 could inform the mobile user the recycling value of their current phone, best offer for an upgrade, what customers like him/her generally preferred upgrading to, and where the nearest store was. While user's personal data and device data was matched against feature preferences of upgrades for similar demographics, user's location data was synchronized with the location database of mobile phone stores.

Summary and Concluding Observations

Mobile data is opening up ever-new possibilities for marketers. There are, of course, tradeoffs—between the convenience that the collection and transmission of such personal data offers consumers; and the control it removes from them, by violating a sense of privacy. Despite all skepticism, the synchronicity value of mobile data is gaining increasing popularity among younger users, who are more functionally dependent on these technologies for their day-to-day tasks, and (compared to older generations) less sensitive about their personal space or territories. Enterprises are taking advantage of this growing opportunity, Uberizing more and more businesses by crowdsourcing delivery processes, by tracking consumer locations real-time. The core platforms of these new businesses are supported by identifiable and location-shared data, and there are multiple entities and ecosystems that benefit from this information. The data can also be stored, anonymized and accessed by third-party data brokers who can generate insights for publishers, advertisers, brands, and other agencies. The vast opportunities of synchronicity need to keep in check the threats to data security. These and other major public policy issues—arising in the Brave New World of pervasive connectivity of people, their devices, and objects all around them—are discussed in the next chapter.

Notes

1. These examples are drawn from Laskowski (2015).

CHAPTER 5

Mobile and Policy Issues

The Electronic Frontier Foundation (EFF), the main public interest group in the United States that has been in existence since 1990 to protect people's privacy and personal data in the electronic age, is blunt in its assessment of the vulnerability and fallibility of mobile phones[1]:

> Mobile phones have become ubiquitous and basic communications tools . . . . Unfortunately, mobile phones were not designed for privacy and security. Not only do they do a poor job of protecting your communications, they also expose you to new kinds of surveillance risks—especially location tracking. Most mobile phones give the user much less control than a personal desktop or laptop computer would . . . .

These problems notwithstanding, because of their overwhelming convenience, mobile phones have swept our world. Before the end of the second decade of the twenty-first century, there will be at least 1.5 mobile phones for every inhabitant of planet Earth. With such a pervasive global technology, the public and private challenges of protecting personal information and security of mobile users are daunting. In addition, the interplay of various interests are complex:

- Consumers and their advocates want adequate privacy and complete security, but also total convenience;
- Marketers want to present their brands in the best possible light to each consumer and this requires substantial inroads into consumers' personal data; and
- Governments seek to balance consumer and marketer interests, but also want national security interests to trump all other interests.

Privacy and security problems with mobile data are rising exponentially as technology, markets, and users increasingly move toward wearable mobile devices and the IoT. With wearables and IoT, massive amount of data is being automatically generated and shared and stored at remote locations—in most cases, with no user consent or the vaguest form of user's permission obtained prior to such data collection. Regulators around the world are beginning to sense the need for greater vigilance about data privacy and security in the IoT age. In the United States, the Federal Trade Commission (FTC)—a major consumer protection agency—reviewed the potential issues of IoT and came to this conclusion[2]:

> The IoT presents numerous benefits to consumers, and has the potential to change the ways consumers interact with technology in fundamental ways. In the future, the Internet of Things is likely to meld the virtual and physical worlds together in ways that are currently difficult to comprehend. From a security and privacy perspective, the predicted pervasive introduction of sensors and devices into currently intimate spaces—such as the home, the car, and with wearables and ingestibles, even the body—poses particular challenges. As physical objects in our everyday lives increasingly detect and share observations about us, consumers will likely want privacy. The [Federal Trade] Commission staff will continue to enforce laws, educate consumers and businesses, and engage with consumer advocates, industry, academics, and other stakeholders involved in the IoT to promote appropriate security and privacy protections. At the same time, we [the FTC] urge further self-regulatory efforts on IoT, along with enactment of data security and broad-based privacy legislation.

In this chapter, we discuss the mobile policy issues under four main headings: privacy issues in general; issues of mobile data ownership and use; data security issues, especially transactional and identity data; and the issues arising from cross-national differences about privacy and security.

With ubiquitous mobile devices, mobile connectivity, mobile data—and around-the-corner and fast-approaching IoT—all the basic principles and core policy issues pertaining to privacy and security require major rethinking. Table 5.1 lays out the well-accepted core principles for protecting the privacy

Table 5.1 Core principles for guiding public policy about mobile privacy and security

Principle	Explanation	Comments
Notice/ Awareness	Consumers and citizens should be aware that personal information is being collected; and they should be given adequate notice of information collection, destination, uses, storage, confidentiality, etc. Notices about data collection should be reasonable and appropriate.	In USA, such information typically exists in paper or electronic fine print, which is typically ignored.
Choice/ Consent	Besides the traditional opt-in/opt-out check boxes, some better methods ask consumers and citizens to prespecify the uses of information that are acceptable to them.	Opt-out has come under fire. Opt-in ways are now more prevalent.
Access	Consumers and citizens should be able to access the data collected about them, and contest the data and/or offer corrections.	In USA, credit bureaus and others offer some redress.
Security	Consumers and citizens should be assured that the data is accurate and secure.	Major data breaches violate this principle.
Transparency	Private entities always, and, under most circumstances, government entities should be open and transparent that they are collecting personal and private data.	Governments can be very secretive, as the Snowden case revealed.
Proportionality	There should be a judicious balancing of the loss of privacy and major risks (such as a terror threat).	This balance keeps shifting, especially when threats arise.
Enforcement	There should be private—and ultimately, public—means to ensure that the principles of personal data privacy and security are enforceable.	European Union (EU) has the strongest public policies and laws in this area.

Source: Authors' framework based on Kranenberg (2008), FTC (2015).

and security of citizens and consumers, principles that guide public policy, especially in the European Union and North America (though national security concerns sometimes overrule some of these in the United States).

Privacy and security issues are going to get more complex with ubiquitous networks, devices, and communications. Data-related challenges will remain—for people in general (in their everyday roles as consumers and citizens) relying increasingly and extensively on mobile devices (and eventually, on connected things), for corporations wanting to offer the best and most competitive offerings, and for governments wanting to ensure technological leadership as well as security. We explore the main areas of concern in the rest of this chapter.

Privacy Issues

In the context of mobile as well as all other forms of electronic communications, issues of privacy arise because all such form of communications generate data: pieces of information that can be accessed, studied, analyzed, responded to, stored, transmitted, distorted, deleted, diverted, hijacked, hacked, stolen, attacked, and more. For any element of mobile data, one can ask:

- Who owns it? To whom does it belong? Who/what does it refer to?
- Who can access it, analyze it, act on it?
- Who can store it, transmit it?
- Who can modify it, blend it with other items, erase it?
- Who can benefit from it, profit from it?
- Who may be harmed or threatened by it?

These are just some sample questions. With the rapid growth in the IoT, the complexity of these issues will increase immensely. In the questions raised above, the underlying assumption is that there is some human actor associated with each data element. In the IoT age, machines and objects will create data and communicate with each other, and thus, the "Who" aspect will either disappear or become very complex—in philosophical, political, cultural, and economic terms.

Layers of Technology in Mobile Communications

For mobile devices to work, multiple layers of technology must work with each other, seamlessly (see Table 5.2). At each layer, there are key actors—usually corporate players, and often, global alliances and consortia—that must have access to key data so that the communications and functions happen smoothly.

Given this layered structure of technologies, a structure that enables mobile phones and devices to do their job, it is important—and quite evident—that data must be shared up and down these layers, for things to happen. The App providers and the OS providers (Apple OS, Android flavor) typically seek very deep and often unlimited and unfettered permissions from the users. In case of OS, it is understandable that such detailed permissions are needed because the OS controls both the on-screen and

Table 5.2 Layers of technology in mobile communications

Technology layer	Examples	Comments
Application	Payment apps, Navigation apps, etc.	The outermost and visible layer. Users give permissions to an app so that the app can work through the OS (see below) to further work with hardware, subscriptions, networks, and third parties
Operating System (OS)	Apple OS, Android	The platform for all the apps, and a bridge between the visible app on the screen and the inner workings of hardware and connected networks.
Hardware	Technological features inside phones, tablets, etc.	Hardware for cellular communications, Wi-Fi, GPS, cameras, processor, memory, display, and more
Subscription	SIM cards or other means to authenticate a device	These enable the devices to connect to and communicate with the wireless operator networks
Networks and Connectivity	Cellular, Wi-Fi, Bluetooth, GPS, NFC	The coverage of the connectivity depends on the method: Wi-Fi, Bluetooth, NFC tend to be local and limited in range, in contrast to cellular networks and GPS

Source: Authors' research.

inner workings of the device. In case of Apps, many observers have found that app developers often want a lot more types of permissions than are needed for the app to do its work. Wi-Fi providers often seek only the device address and IP address, and if it is not free Wi-Fi, then the payment credentials. Cellular network providers, as can be expected, seek a detailed and wide range of permissions from the user.

Mobile privacy protections for U.S. users became weaker in early 2017, via new rules announced by the Federal Communications Commission. Since mobile privacy protections in the European Union remain strong, and were expected to strengthen further, there were possible competitive openings for some European firms to attract U.S. mobile consumers to their platforms. For example:

Telefónica in Germany . . . announced a partnership with U.K. firm People.io to power an app in which the telco giant's customers can control some of their data . . . . The partnership, and Telefóni-ca's approach to handing over more data control to its customers, could serve as a template for what other telcos across the European Union and other markets might do as strict General Data Protection Regulation rules take effect next year [2018] in the EU. The regula-tion, or GDPR, will require companies with data about EU citizens to obtain explicit consent for various data gathering, usage and shar-ing practices . . . . People.io considers its deployment with Telefónica to be the initial stage of its . . . vision . . . "to build a firewall for people." In the future, the company expects people to connect fit-ness trackers, streaming music services or personal finance accounts to the app the way they can attach their email accounts today.[3]

The authors of this book intend to watch closely the cross-Atlantic competitive interplay of privacy issues (especially the GDPR regulation mentioned), and urge the readers of this book to do so as well. EU governments and companies are expected to work at strengthening mobile privacy while the United States adopts a hands-off approach. The issues to watch include the following:

- Will mobile device makers, software firms, and service providers adjust their strategies to conform to the 500 million people of the EU or the 320 million people of the United States?
- Would U.S. firms doing business in and with Europe get into prob-lems because their methods do not conform to the GDPR of the EU?
- Would some EU firms gain as U.S. consumers seek out their plat-forms to safeguard their privacy?

Security Issues

As data elements get shared and distributed up and down these layers, and—eventually, via the networks—get transferred to remote and faceless data clouds, the possibilities of the data getting breached and compro-mised increase. Data security is a constantly moving and shifting target. That is why companies as well as government agencies that specialize in dealing with data security are constantly researching and updating the methods to shield data networks from breaches, the ways to counter threats and attacks when they happen, and the ways to recover from attacks and build up stronger defenses.

Table 5.3 presents a sampling of cybersecurity issues and threats, as of 2017. These, of course, need to be regularly and constantly updated

Table 5.3 A sampling of data security threats and issues

Security threat or issue	Comments
IoT Malware	As everything from baby monitors to thermostats become Internet connected and mobile-enabled, new data breach backdoors will open up and threats will arise for homes and workplaces.
Ransomware	The criminal practice of stealing and locking up someone's data, and releasing it only after a ransom is paid, is rising. Global cooperation to curb this is also growing, holding out hope of curbing such practices.
Cyberattacks, cyberwars	There are growing accusations of these. Soon, a nation would formally accuse another nation of waging cyberwarfare.
Attacks on infrastructure and cloud	These could possibly be at a national level, but even more likely such attacks could be employed to disable and degrade a major competitor.
Criminal use of encryption	National security agencies are already claiming that terrorists and other criminals use encryption to communicate with each other, in undetected ways. Such criminal use of encryption will keep rising.
Fake news and online deception, cyberpropaganda	These already started appearing in major ways in 2016, and the use of such methods will continue to rise.
Use of drones	Drones will be used for espionage and cyberattacks. Conversely, drones will be vulnerable to hacking and be the targets of attacks.
Vulnerability of secure protocols	Formerly secure protocols, such as Secure Socket Layer (SSL) and the HTTPS safe-browsing, will become vulnerable.
Fake 'Likes', fake ads, fake endorsements	These will erode the trust in the reviews that people have come to rely on.
Cyberthefts of money	Not just criminals, but rogue nations may resort to stealing money from financial systems.
Criminal use of AI and machine Learning	Artificial Intelligence (AI) and Machine Learning, generally employed to improve our lives, will find criminal uses.
Vulnerability of voice-activated devices	Voice-activated mobile apps and devices (Siri, Alexa, Cortana) will open up new doorways for criminal hackers and others.

Source: Authors' research, based on Lohrmann (2017) and other sources.

by those working in the fields of mobile communications and mobile commerce and marketing.

A Global Look at Mobile Policy Issues

There are, of course, as many mobile public policy models in the world as the number of national political entities. For example, Vodafone—which runs, often with partners, mobile phone services in almost 80 countries—reported in 2014 that in Albania, Egypt, Hungary, India, Malta, Qatar, Romania, South Africa, and Turkey, the company was prohibited from disclosing whether or not the Vodafone mobile networks were being used for wiretapping of certain mobile phone accounts. In six additional countries—countries that Vodafone refused to name in its report—the company had to give complete access to the governments to the company's mobile networks. These six governments could monitor Vodafone customers whenever they wanted.[4]

Since it is not possible to cover all 200-plus national entities here, we want to focus on mobile public policy issues in three important regions—the European Union (EU), China, and the developing world.

The European Union

In general, for mobile data, the European Union has enacted some of the strongest privacy protection laws in the world. As an example, the $19 billion takeover of the mobile messaging services WhatsApp by Facebook has raised particular concerns with EU regulators. While traditional telecom company services, including SMS-texting, are well-covered by EU regulations, many in the EU believe that WhatsApp services—offered under the guise of social media services—are, in reality, telecom services and should be subject to the same regulations that telecom companies are subject to. EU has also expressed concerns over the sharing of data between Facebook and WhatsApp accounts, and Facebook has promised to keep the two sets of data strictly compartmentalized, for EU-based users.[5]

EU regulations about data security and privacy have very substantial implications for all actors in the mobile ecosystem (see Chapter 1). New

EU regulations, introduced in 2017, bring in several elements of major importance to the mobile sector, including these[6]:

- Separate directives in the EU member countries will get harmonized into a uniform EU-wide regulation.
- Anyone who touches or sees an individual's data, including third parties, could be held accountable if there is a data breach.
- Non-EU organizations (companies, governments, others) who have access to data of EU citizens and residents will also be covered by the new regulation.
- In case of data loss or unlawful use of their data, EU citizens and residents will be able to seek monetary damages from the organization that is held accountable.
- Moving data of EU individuals across countries, particularly to a cloud service outside the EU, may become difficult.
- Individuals in EU will have strong rights to demand data removal or erasure, but this could be very challenging when the data has migrated to, and become distributed across, multiple players and countries.
- Organizations—companies, governments, and others—who collect data about individuals will have to inform such individuals in a comprehensive way, periodically, and seek permission ("opt-in").
- Very heavy fines—up to 5 percent of revenues or 100 million euros, whichever is higher—could be levied for some of the serious violations.
- In most cases, encryption and tokenization of data would protect companies and other organizations from the dangers of data breaches; however, issues of what happens when national security conflicts arise, remain unclear (see Table 5.1).

China

It is no secret that all electronic activity is very likely monitored in China. Indeed, the disclosure by Edward Snowden of massive collection of communications metadata in the United States[7]—a country that constantly champions freedom of expression and freedom from government

Table 5.4 Chinese companies benefiting from the great firewall

Company	Products/ services	Key statistics	Comments
Baidu	Search engine, mapping, e-payments, driverless cars	Nearly 700 million users	Became China's largest and one of world's biggest search engine companies after expulsion of Google in 2010
Huawei	Mobile phones, tablets, network equipment	45 of 50 top global telecom operators use its network equipment	US, UK, and other countries' politicians have raised issues of Huawei devices, equipment likely passing data on to Chinese spy agencies
ZTE	Mobile network equipment, smartphones, IoT, and VR products	2015 revenues exceeded $15 billion and were growing at double-digit rates	US, UK, and other countries' politicians have raised issues of ZTE devices, equipment likely passing data on to Chinese spy agencies
Xiaomi	Mobile phones, android devices, smartphone software, smart set-top boxes	2017 revenue expected to top $17 billion and market valuation could reach $50 billion	Privately held till early 2017, but has attracted funds from top global venture investors. Smart mobile devices often targeted head-to-head with Apple products.
Sina	Social media platform, online content provider, online advertising	90 percent of users access Sina Weibo via mobile devices	Led the social media field in China before the rapid rise of WeChat from Tencent. China's 2016 tightening of censorship rules has affected Sina's Weibo traffic.
Tencent	Messaging, games, e-commerce	WeChat messaging app has 700 million users	Rapidly surpassed Sina Weibo app

Source: Authors' research; based on Abbruzzese (2015), Mullen (2016), and other sources.

interference—was somewhat of a surprise; but in the case of China, no one is surprised by the extent of surveillance. Still, sometimes, the attempts by local police departments in China to tap into mobile phone communications in their cities cause a bit of a surprise, even to the Chinese citizens.[8]

It is well known that to block content that the Chinese government considers politically or culturally unacceptable, the electronic blocking system—generally dubbed as the Great Firewall of China—has been created. Via the use of Virtual Private Networks (VPNs), the users in China are able to get around the great firewall and access outside content, but the hassles and the costs are high: VPN-routed communications are very slow, and also, there are frequent breakdowns because the government censors try to continually shut down or block such channels. Furthermore, laws in China have been tightened to catch and prosecute VPN users. As a result, users in China have largely given up on using VPN-based approaches to access prohibited content. One result of this has been a huge boost in business for Chinese equipment makers and service providers—these companies allow total access to Chinese surveillance authorities and are therefore able to offer high-bandwidth, low-cost, superior services. Table 5.4 lists some of the major indirect corporate beneficiaries of the Great Firewall of China, and these companies are now aggressively entering markets outside China.

The Developing World

We have presented numerous examples in this book about how mobile phone are transforming lives in the less affluent developing world, the set of about 150 countries that account for more than half of the global population. Over the coming several years, millions of mobile users in the developing world are expected to transition from basic phones to smartphones, and from low-bandwidth to high-bandwidth networks.

In general, the protection of personal mobile data in the developing world is poor and the vulnerabilities are high. Table 5.5 lists several examples of problems or potential problems due to poor safeguarding of personal mobile data in the developing nations.

While the problems of protecting mobile data in the developing world are daunting, there are also advantages in the mobile technology sector for many developing countries. The advantages arise from the fact that these countries usually do not have entrenched legacy systems and are often able to build strong mobile tech-based businesses and policies afresh. Table 5.6 provides select illustrations where mobile firms or

Table 5.5 Examples of poor safeguarding of mobile data in developing nations

National context	Mobile data type	Problems, potential problems, difficulties
Haiti	HIV infection data	Government demanded all volunteer health organizations to share HIV data they had about their served populations. No specific protections offered about privacy and use of such data.
India	Military data	India's armed forces have asked their personnel not to use Chinese made Xiaomi mobile phones for fears that sensitive military data may be compromised.
Hong Kong	Mobile malware	When young people in Hong Kong were holding anti-China "Occupy Central" pro-democracy protests, hackers from mainland China, siding with the Chinese authorities, flooded the mobile phones of the Hong Kong protesters with malware.
Indonesia, Nigeria, Tanzania, Kenya	Malware preloaded on new phone sets	Masquerading as a ringtone app, this malware could download SMS and WAP (Wireless Application Protocol) content, including sensitive private information of the phone user.
Peru, Costa Rica, Chile	Jumcar malicious code to target mobile banking apps	The malicious code was used to steal financial information of mobile and PC-based online banking customers, and to access their accounts
India	National Payment Corporation of India (NPCI) data breach	3.2 million debit cards in India, linked to NCPI, were being used illegally. Data breach originated from an ATM malware.

Source: Authors' compilation from multiple sources, including Bernard (2015); Hussain (2015); Prince (2014).

mobile policies can be more forward-looking and proactive than their counterparts in the economically advanced nations.

The developing countries, in principle, may be in a strong position to avoid many of the mobile data privacy and security problems, simply because such data has not existed in legacy systems. In practice, however, we can expect a lot of heterogeneity in the foreseeable future—it is the most proactive policymakers, social service organizations, and companies in the developing world that will come out ahead in the mobile services sphere.

Table 5.6 Examples of proactive mobile tech in developing nations

National context	Example or illustration	Comments
India	CarDekho: Online car buying and selling information and research portal	Car buying, especially new car buying, entails an intense and long digital journey, to research the cars, for growing proportion of car buyers in India. CarDekho provides auto aggregator websites, connecting users—most using mobile devices—to relevant information about available new and used cars.
South Africa	Snapscan: Mobile payment system	To induce early use, teams from the company went to local farmer's markets to facilitate payments, and even to church services to facilitate giving to the church's donation plate.
Colombia	Nequi: Mobile banking service with biometric identification	Launched by Bancolombia, the system allows users to authenticate themselves via selfie pictures (facial recognition software) or voice recognition on their mobile devices.
Tunisia	e-Dinar, Monetas: National electronic currency, e-payment system	Using smartphones, Tunisians are able to do mobile money transfers, pay for goods and services online and in person, send remittances, pay salaries and bills, and manage official government identification documents. Using the blockchain cryptographic technology (on which Bitcoin is based), Tunisia is the first nation to provide such high-level security.
India	Aadhaar: Biometric identification program of Indian government	Almost 100% of Indians over 18 have the Aadhaar biometric identification card, linking nearly 400 million bank accounts, and facilitating over 3 million transactions every day.
Vietnam	Lozi: Food location app, evolving into full-blown e-commerce app	Lozi suggests food spots to users via food pictures from foodie people signed on to the Lozi platform. Users can create own favorite food albums, upload food pictures, and explore off-the-beaten-path food spots.

Source: Authors' compilation from multiple sources, including Mohile (2017); Parussini (2017); Simons (2016); Andreasyan (2016); and Smart (2015).

Safeguarding Privacy, Ensuring Security

As the quote from the Federal Trade Commission (FTC) report at the beginning of this chapter indicated, the issue of personal data protection and privacy needs to be tackled in multipronged ways—through

forward-thinking public policies and government regulations, via
responsible self-regulation by industry actors, and finally and ultimately,
via the vigilant efforts of consumers themselves. While no completely
foolproof methods exist—and the "bad guys" such as malicious hack-
ers and thieves will always look for ways to invade people's privacy—it
is nonetheless important for smart mobile users to be aware of ways to
protect their data and themselves. In a constantly changing and evolving mobile world, it is impossible to create a list of safeguards that is
totally comprehensive or invulnerable. Nonetheless, it is useful for all
mobile users to start building their own strategies to guard themselves
against privacy and security breaches. The following building blocks are
a start, and users should continually update and upgrade, commencing
from these basics:

- Mobile users should establish strong passwords that cannot be
  guessed or spoofed easily.
- It is important to have a trusted antivirus app, to protect the mobile
  device from malicious apps. Some estimates indicate that 1 in 3 apps
  available may have malicious elements or other vulnerabilities.
- Activities requiring high security—banking, e-commerce, e-mail,
  and so on—should be avoided or kept to a minimum when the
  mobile device is using a Wi-Fi network, except in those cases where
  the service being used guarantees strict data encryption.
- When a device is unlocked in an unauthorized way, it is likely to
  become vulnerable to data breaches and privacy threats.
- When links or apps are clicked on from untrusted e-mails or sites,
  the vulnerability is high.
- It is best to stick to official app sources, such as Apple Store and
  Google Play. Third-party app sites and other sources could intro-
  duce vulnerabilities.
- Mobile users should carefully study the various permissions they
  are granting to device makers, operating systems, mobile network
  operators, Wi-Fi access providers, app developers and managers, social media platforms, and others. This is an onerous task,
  and—except very security-conscious and technically sophisticated

users—most people are likely to slack off with respect to the permissions that they grant.

- For higher and stronger security, experts recommend several things: (a) disabling location tracking; (b) using anonymizer sites to do browsing of sites; (c) regularly updating the device's operating system; (d) using back-up apps to back-up the data on the mobile devices. Of course, this also implies missing out on the convenience of things such as location-based services and offers as well as personalized and tailored ways of getting services.

- In case of the device being lost or stolen, it is useful to install a remote wipe app that can be activated remotely to wipe clean the data on the lost device. Also, a screen lock password would deter an unauthorized user from accessing the device.

Concluding Observations

Several factors point to increasing complexity and a growing range of challenges in terms of dealing with the mobile privacy and security. Geopolitical factors seem to be evolving in ways that threaten the privacy and security of data, be it the data of ordinary private individuals or of corporations or of organizations (such as political parties or nonprofit agencies), and even the data of powerful government agencies. Technological capabilities that make life interesting, convenient, and enjoyable for mobile users also typically have a darker side. This is because technologies to probe, hack, disrupt, and destroy are also evolving at a rapid pace.[9]

Many governments are concerned about the threats to privacy, and the rising breaches of data security. They are formulating regulations that impose strict controls on data storage and flows, and are enacting stiff penalties for violators. Like any field with potential for unethical behavior and/or deliberate criminality, however, the field of mobile communications is going to remain a contested one. The good guys—citizen and consumer protection groups and forward-thinking governments—will keep trying to shield people and organizations, while the bad guys (unethical companies, cybercriminals) will continue to seek ways to make money in nefarious ways through misuse or stealing of mobile data.

Notes

1. Quote is from EFF (2015).
2. Quote is from FTC (2015).
3. Quote is from an article by Kate Kaye (2017) in *Advertising Age*.
4. See BBC (2014) for more details.
5. See Essers (2015); Fioretti (2016); Vincent (2014).
6. Based on Hawthorn (2015).
7. See Ball (2013); Gellman and Soltani (2013).
8. See, for example, Chan (2011).
9. See, for example, Kshetri (2016).

Epilogue

Back to the Future

The chapters presented in this book elaborate on the opportunities marketers can explore to reach and react to technologically connected consumers. Mobile technology has been a planet-wide turning point—raising both marketer capabilities as well as quality of consumer access and experience with the marketplace, in countries rich as well as those striving to develop economically. The explosion of data availability and deployment of algorithms for daily tasks is likely to evolve the mobile markets, in terms of behaviors and strategies, in ways that are difficult to project and predict. Yet, marketers as well as consumers need some guide-posts as to what the future may hold.

The Unfolding IoT Future

Mobile device use, ubiquitous consumer interactions and exchange, and marketer-drawn insights are merely the tip of the iceberg. Internet of Things (IoT) are expected to regularize the mass deployment of ubiquitous sensors through, products, possessions, assets and everyday items, leading to greater interactivity by seamless data transmission from home security systems, refrigerators in household electronics, showers, cars, dog collars in lifestyle products, cattle and livestock in agriculture, among many others. The storage, analysis, and triangulation of such information for improving the efficiency and quality of operations and experiences can use the conceptual and analytical frameworks presented in this book for location-based mobile data as a stepping-stone for dynamic synchronization.

As marketers learn dynamically about occupied/vacant spaces (kitchen, bedroom, and bathroom) within a household, the mobile-based home systems can synchronize lighting, temperature, and music accordingly. As marketers learn about fluctuating biometrics, the mobile health-oriented systems can recommend—according to the continually monitored biometrics—the appropriately nutritious consumable grocery items. As the refrigerator learns about milk inventory running below a threshold, it can automatically place a reorder for it. Keeping pace with upcoming opportunities are the challenges.

Increasing Complexity of Privacy–Security Challenges

To protect consumer privacy and shared data, which is the fulcrum for the all the revolutionary changes mentioned, several legislative bills have been proposed or passed in the United States. The most significant among them—that directly address mobile devices—are related to geolocation data. The Geolocation Privacy and Surveillance Act (2013), Online Communications and Geolocation Protection Act (2013–2014) and the Location Privacy Protection Act of 2014 are some important examples. Similarly, location-based data is a part of personal information under Australia's Privacy Act, from which individual identity can be determined despite the process being lengthy and complex.

On the other extreme, trends in electronic discovery are allowing more and more of location-based data to be used in the courtroom for civil or criminal proceedings, and location data of users from manufacturers of mobile or wearable devices can become accessible as public information. In March 2015, police from Lancaster, Pennsylvania, used evidence from a defendant's wearable fitness device to contradict a statement (alleged that she was sleeping), as her wearable fitness tracker showed that she was awake and active, and proved that she was staging a fake crime scene. The data broker industry is compiling user information for third-party use, and the third parties can be any entities from grocery retailers to pharmaceutical manufacturers, as well as medical establishments. Of course, doors also open up for the use of such data by criminals or unwarranted state surveillance bodies.

The deeper problem is that most legislation offers protection based on consumers' consent. With increasing abundance of information, or information overload, consumers are absorbing and comprehending less information than they have access to, avoiding processing effort, and compromising the whole notion of "informed" consent. Unconscious approvals are meaningless if they mean to confer legal validity to actions that, with due deliberation, people may not consent to.

Fundamental Transformations

For marketers, there is a larger consumer behavior transformation underway. Earlier, most marketers were themselves concerned with whether consumers are making rational or irrational decisions. With the increased availability of smart engines and data-driven tools and algorithms, today's consumers can make rational/irrational decisions in both conscious and unconscious manners. Increasingly, consumers may act in ways such that their decision processes and outcomes may appear rational, but are truly outsourced to artificial intelligent processes. That is likely to change who plays the influencer and decision-maker roles in choice processes. At present, the conceptual and practical frameworks presume that there is consent, deliberation, free will, and conscious processing of information and making of decisions. In the future, with the changed roles played by mobile and IoT, seamless consumers may need marketers to change their target audiences and objects for persuasion. Half-funny and half-scary, it may be easier or more worthwhile to persuade a smart mirror in the bathroom—rather than the consumer herself—to nudge her to try an antiwrinkle cream. Or, to use another scenario, a smart connected car, sensing a user's poor health condition via biometric sensors, may override the user's desire to go to a sports bar for "beer and wings," and take him to a workout gym instead.

What the future holds, in terms of mobile and ubiquitously connected technologies, would transform not just marketing and business, but a host of fundamental fields, such as psychology, medicine, law, and even philosophy.

Bibliography

The following listing contains all the sources mentioned in the book and the endnotes, as well as additional sources. Interested readers are encouraged to explore all these sources, as well as the resources available from the three authors available at sites such as ResearchGate, Academia.edu, Kudos, Wikipedia, and LinkedIn. Readers wishing to follow up further should search at such sites, using the names of the three authors. Interested readers and researchers should also seek the help of professional bibliographic experts at their libraries to seek additional sources and information.

Abbruzzese, Jason (2015), "What Is Xiaomi? Getting to Know the Chinese Company That Is Taking on Apple", *Mashable*, January 18, Available at: https://goo.gl/LQgBvE, Accessed: February 11, 2017.

Andreasyan, Tanya (2016), "Bancolombia's Nequi First in Colombia to Deploy Mobile Biometrics", *Banking Technology*, August 31, Available at: https://goo.gl/auKLHN, Accessed: March 7, 2017.

Arruda-Filho, Emílio J.M., Julianne A. Cabusas, and Nikhilesh Dholakia (2010), "Social Behavior and Brand Devotion among iPhone Innovators", *International Journal of Information Management* 30 (6): 475–480.

Ball, James (2013), "NSA Stores Metadata of Millions of Web Users for up to a Year, Secret Files Show", *The Guardian*, September 30, Available at: https://goo.gl/5MDASA, Accessed:

Banerjee, Syagnik and Philip Longstreet (2016), "Mind in eBay, Body in Macy's: Dual Consciousness of Virtuo-physical Consumers and Implications for Marketers", *Journal of Research in Interactive Marketing*, 10 (4): 288–304.

Banerjee, Syagnik, Amit Poddar, Scott Yancy, and Danielle McDowell (2011), "Measuring Intangible Effects of m-Coupon Campaigns on Non-redeemers", *Journal of Research in Interactive Marketing*, 5 (4), 258–275.

Banerjee, Syagnik and Fareena Sultan (2016), "Social Media Geoforensics: An Exploratory Analysis", *Direct/Interactive Marketing Research Summit, Los Angeles, CA*, October 15–16, 2016.

Banerjee, Syagnik and Rishika Rishika (2015), "The Art of Mistiming: How Interruptions Make Mobile Coupon Campaigns Effective", *Journal of Direct, Data and Digital Marketing Practice,* December, 17 (2): 101–113.

Banerjee, Syagnik [Sy] and Ruby Roy Dholakia (2008), "Mobile Advertising: Does Location Based Advertising Work?" *International Journal of Mobile Marketing*, 6 (3): 68–74.

Banerjee, Syagnik and Ruby Roy Dholakia (2009), "Convenient or Intrusive? The Role of "When" and "Where" in Consumer Reactions to Mobile Advertising", *AP-Asia-Pacific Advances in Consumer Research*, 8: 213–214.

Banerjee, Syagnik and Ruby Roy Dholakia (2012), "Location Based Mobile Advertisements and Gender Targeting", *Journal of Research in Interactive Marketing*, 6 (3): 198–214.

Banerjee, Syagnik and Ruby Roy Dholakia (2013), "Situated or Ubiquitous? A Segmentation of Mobile e-Shoppers", *International Journal of Mobile Communications*, 11 (5): 530–557.

Banerjee, Syagnik, Vijay Viswanathan, Kalyan Raman, and Hao Ying (2013), "Assessing Prime-Time for Geotargeting with Mobile Big Data", *Journal of Marketing Analytics*, 1 (3): 174–183.

Banerjee, Syagnik and Scott Yancy (2010), "Enhancing Mobile Coupon Redemption in Fast Food Campaigns", *Journal of Research in Interactive Marketing*, 4 (2): 97–110.

BBC (2014), "Vodafone Reveals Direct Government Wiretaps", *BBC News Online—Business*, June 6, Available at: https://goo.gl/4v2Fwl, Accessed: February 17, 2017.

Bernard, Doug (2015), "How to Safeguard Your Mobile Privacy", *Voice of America*, May 15, Available at: http://goo.gl/XX0GHb, Accessed: December 19, 2016.

Bhattacharya, Pramit (2016), "99% Indian Households are Covered by a Bank Account", *Livemint*, December 15, Available at: http://goo.gl/SXdu42 , Accessed: August 28, 2017.

Boden, Rian (2017), "Banco Bradesco Customers Get Mobile-Only Banking", *NFC World*, June 8, Available at: https://goo.gl/fslFKD, Accessed: December 19, 2016.

Chan, Casey (2011), "China Wants to Track Its Citizens by Tapping into Their Cell Phones", *Gizmodo*, March 3, Available at: https://goo.gl/5ph3Y6, Accessed: July 12, 2016.

Chirgwin, Richard (2015), "Even China's Academy of Science Thinks Wearables Are Privacy Problem", *The Register*, January 5, Available at: http://goo.gl/yj5L6b, Accessed: March 7, 2017.

CISCO (2015), "Cisco Visual Networking Index: Global Mobile Data Traffic Forecast Update 2014–2019 White Paper", February 3, Available at: http://goo.gl/J2ShCj, Accessed: September 23, 2016.

Dean, Jeffrey and Sanjay Ghemawat (2008), "MapReduce: Simplified Data Processing on Large Clusters", *Communications of the ACM*, 51 (1): 107–113.

Dholakia, Nikhilesh, Morten Rask, and Ruby Roy Dholakia, eds. (2006), *M-Commerce: Global Experiences and Perspectives*, Hershey PA: IGI Global.

Dholakia, Nikhilesh and Nir Kshetri (2002), "The Global Digital Divide and Mobile Business Models: Identifying Viable Patterns of e-Development", In *Proceedings of the Seventh IFIP WG9. 4 Conference*, Bangalore, India, May 29–31.

Dholakia, Nikhilesh and Nir Kshetri (2003), "Mobile Commerce As a Solution to the Global Digital Divide: Selected Cases of e-Development". Available at: https://goo.gl/ZlaOxo, Accessed: May 15, 2017.

Dholakia, Nikhilesh and Detlev Zwick (2003), "Mobile Technologies and Boundaryless Spaces: Slavish Lifestyles, Seductive Meanderings, or Creative Empowerment?", *H.O.I.T. 2003: The Networked Home and the Home of the Future*, University of California, Irvine, April 7, Available at: https://goo.gl/LQenE1, Accessed: May 15, 2017.

Dholakia, Nikhilesh and Detlev Zwick (2004), "Cultural Contradictions of the Anytime, Anywhere Economy: Reframing Communication Technology", *Telematics and Informatics*, 21 (2): 123–141.

Dholakia, Nikhilesh, Ruby Roy Dholakia, Mark Lehrer, and Nir Kshetri (2004), "Global Heterogeneity in the Emerging m-Commerce Landscape", *Wireless Communications and Mobile Commerce*, edited by Nan Si Shi, Hershey PA: Idea Group Publishing, 1–22.

Dholakia, Ruby Roy (2012), *Technology and Consumption: Understanding Consumer Choices and Behaviors*, New York: Springer Science & Business Media.

Dholakia, Ruby Roy and Kuan-Pin Chiang (2003), "Shoppers in Cyberspace: Are They From Venus or Mars and Does It Matter?" *Journal of Consumer Psychology,* 13 (1–2): 171–176.

Dholakia, Ruby Roy and Nikhilesh Dholakia (2004), "Mobility and Markets: Emerging Outlines of m-Commerce", *Journal of Business research,* 57 (12): 1391–1396.

Dholakia, Ruby Roy, Norbert Mundorf, and Nikhilesh Dholakia (2013). *New Infotainment Technologies in the Home: Demand-Side Perspectives.* New York and London: Routledge.

Dholakia, Ruby Roy and Outi Uusitalo (2002), "Switching to Electronic Stores: Consumer Characteristics and the Perception of Shopping Benefits." *International Journal of Retail & Distribution Management,* 30 (10): 459–469.

Economist (2013), "Why Does Kenya Lead the World in Mobile Money?" *The Economist,* May 27, Available at: http://goo.gl/i5qE1Z, Accessed: November 11, 2016.

EFF (2015), "The Problem with Mobile Phones", Electronic Frontier Foundation (EFF), February 10, Available at: https://goo.gl/4xvjBM, Accessed: April 22, 2017.

Essers, Loek (2015), "EU Data Protection Authorities Get Serious about Facebook's Privacy Policy", *PCWorld,* February 4, Available at: http://goo.gl/cuuq3G

Evans, D. (2011), "The Internet of Things: How the Next Evolution of the Internet Is Changing Everything", *Cisco, IBSG,* Retrieved from http://www.cisco.com/c/dam/en_us/about/ac79/docs/innov/IoT_IBSG_0411FINAL.pdf

Filloon, Whitney (2016), "UberEats, Amazon Vying for Global Food Delivery Domination", Eater, September 27, Available at: https://goo.gl/RcUHjs, Accessed: May 17, 2017.

Fioretti, Julie (2016), "EU accuses Facebook of Misleading It in WhatsApp Takeover Probe", Reuters, December 16, Available at: https://goo.gl/OFVsRU, Accessed: May 17, 2017.

Fortin, David R. and Ruby Roy Dholakia (2005), "Interactivity and Vividness Effects on Social Presence and Involvement with a Web-Based Advertisement", *Journal of Business Research,* 58 (3): 387–396.

FTC (2015), *Internet of Things: Privacy & Security in a Connected World*, FTC Staff Report, January 2015, Washington DC: Federal Trade Commission.

Fung, Brian (2017), "Amazon Has a Patent to Keep You from Comparison Shopping while You're in Its Stores", *The Washington Post*, June 16, Available at: https://goo.gl/rp2tqc, Accessed: June 17, 2017.

Gellman, Barton and Ashkan Soltani (2013), "NSA Tracking Cellphone Locations Worldwide, Snowden Documents Show", *The Washington Post*, December 4, Available at: https://goo.gl/jy4Az3, Accessed: April 22, 2017.

Grennan, Todd (2017), "How Urban Outfitters Boosted Opens by 100+% and Lifted Conversions by 75%", *Relate* (digital magazine), February 28, Available at: https://goo.gl/6MNtWh, Accessed: April 22, 2017.

Hawthorn, Nigel (2015), "10 Things You Need to Know about the New EU Data Protection Regulation", *COMPUTERWORLDUK*, May 6, Available at: https://goo.gl/B0Yq33, Accessed: September 19, 2016.

Heaton, Alex (2014), "10 Examples of Effective Mobile Business Apps", *Smart Insights*, July 21, Available at: http://goo.gl/yOZnqE, Accessed: February 18, 2017.

Hussain, Hibah (2015), "Cellphone Projects in Developing World Need Better Privacy, Security Measures", *Slate*, May 18, Available at: http://goo.gl/Eae19W, Accessed: March 7, 2017.

Jarboe, Greg (2015), "Mobile Marketing Done Right: 2 Masterful Case Studies", *Momentology*, April 23, Available at: http://goo.gl/BOi0T7, Accessed: November 3, 2016.

Kaye, Kate (2017), "Wave of the Future? Telefonica Gives Consumers Control Over (Some) Mobile Data", *Advertising Age*, May 5, Available at: https://goo.gl/WzBauR, Accessed: June 17, 2017.

Kerrigan, Finola and Andrew Hart (2016), "Theorising Digital Personhood: A Dramaturgical Approach", *Journal of Marketing Management*, 32 (17–18): 1701–1721.

Kirkpatrick, David (2011), "Mobile Marketing: How Redbox Drove 1.5 Million Texts and Added 200,000 Mobile Participants in 10 Days", *MarketingSherpa*, October 6, Available at: https://goo.gl/QdlfBM, Accessed: December 9, 2016.

Kranenberg, Rob van (2008), "Internet of Things: A Critique of Ambient Technology and the All-Seeing Network of RFID", *Makezine*, October 3, Available at: https://goo.gl/U1MLYX, Accessed: February 11, 2017.

Kshetri, Nir (2016), "Cybersecurity and Development", *Markets, Globalization & Development Review*, 1 (2): Article 3.

Kshetri, Nir and Nikhilesh Dholakia (2001), "Impact of Cultural and Political Factors on the Adoption of Digital Signatures in Asia", *AMCIS 2001 Proceedings*: 321.

Lam, Oiwan (2015), "Chinese Police Are Buying Spyware—And Posting Their Purchase Orders Online", *GlobalVoices Advocacy*, January 7, Available at: http://goo.gl/JYTReA, Accessed: March 7, 2017.

Leanplum (2017), "Leanplum Reveals 120 Power Words That Boost Push Notification Engagement & Conversions", *PR Newswire*, May 3, Available at: https://goo.gl/lkXsy3, Accessed: June 17, 2017.

Lehrer, Mark, Nikhilesh Dholakia, and Nir Kshetri (2002), "National Sources of Leadership in 3G m-Business Applications: A Framework and Evidence from Three Global Regions", Available at: https://goo.gl/1JRt0P, Accessed: March 7, 2017.

Lohrmann, Dan (2017), "The Top 17 Security Predictions for 2017", *Government Technology*, January 8, Available at: https://goo.gl/iUYzbz, Accessed: June 17, 2017.

Lonsdale, Chris (2001), "Locked-In to Supplier Dominance: On the Dangers of Asset Specificity for the Outsourcing Decision", *Journal of Supply Chain Management,* 37 (1): 22–27.

Ma, Alexandra (2012), "A Sad Number of Americans Sleep with Their Smartphone in Their Hand", *Huffington Post*, June 29, Available at: http://goo.gl/kFLBKc, Accessed: December 9, 2016.

MarketAndMarkets.com (2016), "Market for Proximity Marketing by Location (Indoor and Outdoor), Technology (Wi-Fi, BLE Beacons, NFC, GPS Geofencing), Hardware (Sensors, RFID Tags), Software (Location Analytics), Service, Application—Global Forecast to 2022" Retrieved from: https://goo.gl/OmLqEb, Accessed: January 21, 2017.

Mohile, Shally Seth (2017), "Auto Aggregator Portals Fueling Online Car Research: BCG-CarDekho Study", *Livemint*, February 28, Available at: https://goo.gl/Y5ZP1V, Accessed: March 7, 2017.

Moth, David (2015), "Six Useful Mobile Marketing Case Studies", *Econsultancy*, March 6, Available at: https://goo.gl/PRnkqT, Accessed: May 15, 2017.

Mullen, Jethro (2016), "Meet China's Tech Behemoths", *CNNtech*, May 17, Available at: https://goo.gl/tXwGSI, Accessed: February 3, 2017.

Parussini, Gabriele (2017), "India's Massive Biometric Identification Program", *Wall Street Journal*, January 13, Available at: https://goo.gl/PdC3P6, Accessed: June 17, 2017.

Poddar, Amit, Syagnik Banerjee, and Karthik Sridhar (2017), "False advertising or slander? Using location based tweets to assess online rating-reliability," *Journal of Business Research*.

Prince, Brian (2014), "Malware Found Pre-loaded on Phones Sold in Asia, Africa: Research", *SecurityWeek*, December 4, Available at: http://goo.gl/1bzJvs, Accessed: November 2, 2016

Quint, Matthew, David Rogers and Rick Ferguson (2013), "Showrooming and the rise of the mobile-assisted shopper." *Columbia Business School: Center on Global Brand Leadership*, 9: 1–36.

Rask, Morten and Nikhilesh Dholakia (2001), "Next to the Customer's Heart And Wallet: Frameworks for Exploring the Emerging m-Commerce Arena", *American Marketing Association Conference Proceedings*, 12: 372.

Reyes, Ian, Nikhilesh Dholakia, and Jennifer K. Bonoff (2015), "Disconnected/Connected: On the 'Look' and the 'Gaze' of Cell Phones", *Marketing Theory*, 15 (1): 113–127.

Riordan, Michael H. and Oliver E. Williamson (1985), "Asset Specificity and Economic Organization", *International Journal of Industrial Organization*, 3 (4): 365–378.

Rybarczyk, Greg and Syagnik Banerjee (2015), "Visualizing Active Travel Sentiment in an Urban Context", *Journal of Transport and Health*, 2 (2) S30.

Sanborn, Randall, Michael Farmer, and Syagnik Banerjee (2015), "Assigning Geo-relevance of Sentiments Mined from Location-Based Social Media Posts", *Advances in Intelligent Data Analysis*, Saint Etienne, France, Volume: XIV, October.

Scott, Mark (2015), "As Facebook Sweeps across Europe, Regulators Gird for Battle", *New York Times*, May 25, Available at: http://goo.gl/s1FMCd, Accessed: February 11, 2017.

Simons, Hadlee (2016), "What We Learnt from Snapscan at MTN's App Breakfast", *Ventureburn*, July 4, Available at: https://goo.gl/SmY22I, Accessed: April 25, 2017.

Singh, Manish (2017), "Facebook launches Express Wi-Fi in India, Offers Affordable, Fast Internet to Millions", *Mashable*, May 4, Available at: https://goo.gl/30arH8, Accessed: June 17, 2017.

Smart, Evander (2015), "Tunisia Becomes First Nation to Put Nation's Currency on a Blockchain", *DCEBrief*, December 28, Available at: https://goo.gl/6Hg8Mw, Accessed: December 12, 2016.

Stern, Neil (2017), "The Impact of The Amazon-Whole Foods Deal Will Go Far Beyond Food", *Forbes*, June 20, Available at: https://goo.gl/v8QVLF, Accessed: June 25, 2017.

Tiongson, James (2015), "Mobile App Marketing Insights: How Consumers Really Find and Use Your Apps", Think with Google, May, Available at: https://goo.gl/hK4JKT, Accessed: August 30, 2017.

Vincent, Michael (2014), "Vodafone's Disclosure Report Reveals Global Scale of Mobile Phone Surveillance", *ABC—Australian Broadcasting Corporation*, June 6, Available at: http://goo.gl/FecJub, Accessed: March 7, 2017.

Watercutter, Angela (2013), "How Oreo Won the Marketing Super Bowl with a Timely Blackout Ad on Twitter", *Wired*, February 4, Available at: http://goo.gl/CwfgmB, Accessed: February 11, 2017.

Weise, Karen (2014), "The Do-Good Startups of Nairobi", *Bloomberg Businessweek*, December 29, Available at: http://goo.gl/OjtDIc, Accessed: April 24, 2017.

Zhang, Mann (Michael) (2016), "Virtual Goods Markets and Economy in China: A Historic Account", *Markets, Globalization & Development Review*, 1 (1): Article 7.

Zwick, Detlev and Nikhilesh Dholakia (2004), "Whose Identity Is It Anyway? Consumer Representation in the Age of Database Marketing", *Journal of Macromarketing*, 24 (1): 31–43.

About the Authors

Syagnik 'Sy' Banerjee

Syagnik Banerjee ("Sy") is an Associate Professor of Marketing at University of Michigan - Flint. He has been a pioneer in research on the impact of mobile devices in digital marketing, consumer insights, and behavior. His research covers areas including the Effectiveness of Mobile Advertising, Patterns of Wireless Internet Use, Social Media Listening, Consumer Practices with Internet of Things (IOT), and Analysis of Location-Based Big Data. Prior to joining academia, he worked for four intense years in rural marketing in the areas of sales, distribution, and supply chain management with fast moving consumer goods and telecommunication industries.

He developed the first academic course on mobile interactive marketing and offered it for Northwestern University, was guest speaker at the Mobile University Summit (Chicago), Mobile Media Summit (Chicago), and has been a collaborator with Heartland Mobile Council (Chicago) for developing a certification program for mobile marketers. He has helped the UM Flint School of Management win the Community One Awards from MMBDC through his teaching and the OakGov challenge with AT&T through his research efforts. He has developed a Digital Marketing course for MBA students, and created in-house mobile applications for extracting and synthesizing location-based mobile data. He has also offered a one-day workshop on mobile marketing for industry executives at the International Management Institute, Kolkata.

He has published in *Journal of Business Research, Journal of Research in Interactive Marketing,* and *Journal of Marketing Analytics,* among several others. He is a member of the Collaborative Neuro-marketing Group at Northwestern University and an affiliate faculty member at the Michigan Institute of Data Sciences (MIDAS). He serves as reviewer for American Marketing Association (AMA) Summer Educators Conference, Association for Consumer Research (ACR), *Decision Sciences, Journal of Interactive*

Marketing, European Journal of Marketing, Journal of Research in Interactive Marketing, and *Global Business Review.* He received his PhD in Business (Marketing) from the University of Rhode Island, MBA (Marketing) from International Management Institute, New Delhi, India, and his Bachelor in Science (Economics) from Presidency College, Kolkata, India.

Ruby Roy Dholakia

Ruby Roy Dholakia ("Ruby") is Professor of Marketing and was the Founder and Director of the Research Institute for Telecommunications and Information Marketing (RITIM), in the College of Business Administration at the University of Rhode Island (URI) in the United States. She has also been a full-time faculty as well as Visiting Professor at the Indian Institute of Management – Calcutta (IIMC) and the Indian Institute of Management – Ahmedabad (IIMA). She holds a BS in Marketing, an MBA from the Haas School at University of California at Berkeley, and PhD in Marketing from the Kellogg School at Northwestern University. She has taught at Kansas State University (USA).

Research and consulting projects of RITIM have been supported by AT&T, Verizon, Bellcore, Telecom Italia, Motorola, Rhode Island Public Utilities Commission, and Unisys.

She has been a visiting faculty at the Norwegian Institute of Marketing Research, a visiting scholar at the Haas School of Business at the University of California, Berkeley, a visiting professor at Chuo University, Japan and at University of Jyväskylä, Finland; and at XLRI, IIMA, and IIMC in India; and an Erskine Fellow at University of Canterbury, New Zealand.

Engaged extensively in research projects on technologies for the home, the retail environment, and the workplace, she has chaired several conferences and special sessions on related topics. Her research has been presented to various audiences, business and academic, in the United States, Asia, Western Europe, and Latin America. Her books include *Marketing Strategies for Information Technologies* (JAI Press, 1994), *New Infotainment Technologies in the Home: Demand-Side Perspectives* (Lawrence Erlbaum Associates, 1996), *Worldwide E-Commerce and Online Marketing: Watching the Evolution* (Quorum, 2003), *Marketing Practices in Developing Economy: Cases from South Asia* (Prentice-Hall

India 2009), and *Technology and Consumption: Understanding Consumer Choices and Behaviors* (Springer, 2012).

Her research has appeared in several international journals, such as *Journal of Consumer Research, Public Opinion Quarterly, Journal of Business Research, European Journal of Marketing, Journal of Macromarketing, Journal of Consumer Psychology*, and *Journal of Interactive Marketing.*

She served on the Editorial Policy Board of the *Journal of Macromarketing* and was the first President of the International Society for Markets and Development (ISMD). In 2017, Ruby won the URI Foundation Scholarly Excellence Award as well as the Sheila Grubman Black Award for faculty service from the URI Faculty Senate and the URI President's Office. More details about her research and publications can be found via her Google Scholar page.

Nikhilesh Dholakia

Nikhilesh Dholakia ("Nik Dholakia") is a global author, research scholar, and consultant based in Rhode Island, USA. He is Professor Emeritus from the University of Rhode Island (URI) and the founding co-editor of the online, peer reviewed, open access journal *Markets, Globalization & Development Review.* He has also taught at the University of Illinois at Chicago, Kansas State University, and Indian Institutes of Management at Ahmedabad and Calcutta. He has been a visiting faculty at Northwestern University's Kellogg School, Chuo University in Japan, Arizona State University West, University of Southern Denmark (Odense), Aalto University (Helsinki) School of Economics and Business, Le Havre University in France, Norwegian Institute for Market Research, and Aalborg University in Denmark, and an Erskine Fellow at the University of Christchurch, New Zealand.

Nik Dholakia's research deals with the intersections of globalization, technology, innovation, market processes, and consumer culture. He has worked on projects on Organization Buying of Telecom Systems, Global Telecom Markets, Information Technology in the Home, Technology Adoption and Diffusion Processes, Global Development of Markets for Addressable Television Systems, Privacy Issues on the Internet, Public Policy toward Telecommunications, Asian Road-based

Transport, Metaverse Identities, Globalization of Indian Businesses, Global Transportation Networks & Supply Chains, Retailing in India and Asia, and Social Media.

Among his books are *Essentials of New Product Management* (Prentice-Hall, 1987), *Consumption and Marketing: Macro Dimensions* (South-Western, 1996), *New Infotainment Technologies in the Home: Demand-Side Perspectives* (Lawrence Erlbaum Associates, 1996), *Consuming People: From Political Economy to Theaters of Consumption* (Routledge, 1998), *Worldwide E-Commerce and Online Marketing: Watching the Evolution* (Quorum, 2002), *M-commerce: Global Experiences and Perspectives* (Idea Group Publishing, 2006), and *Toward a Metatheory of Economic Bubbles: Socio-Political and Cultural Perspectives* (Palgrave Macmillan, 2014).

Articles authored by him have appeared in, among other places, *Journal of International Management, Journal of Marketing, Journal of Marketing Management, Marketing Theory, Consumption Markets & Culture, Columbia Journal of World Business, Journal of the Academy of Marketing Science, European Journal of Marketing, Journal of Business Research, Journal of Interactive Marketing, Journal of Macromarketing, Qualitative Market Research, Journal of Electronic Commerce in Organiza-tions, Electronic Market*s and *Information & Organization*.

Nik Dholakia has been a co-winner of the Charles Slater award for the *Journal of Macromarketing*. He has also chaired doctoral dissertations that have won the MSI/Clayton and ACR/Sheth Foundation awards.

Nik holds a B.Tech in Chemical Engineering from the Indian Institute of Technology at Delhi (IIT-Delhi), an MBA from the Indian Institute of Management at Ahmedabad (IIMA), and a PhD in Marketing from the Kellogg School at Northwestern University.

His research can be followed via Google Scholar, ResearchGate, Academia.edu and Kudos.

Index

OTHER TITLES IN DIGITAL AND SOCIAL MEDIA MARKETING AND ADVERTISING COLLECTION

Victoria L. Crittenden, Babson College, *Editor*

- *Mobile Commerce: How It Contrasts, Challenges and Enhances Electronic Commerce* by Esther Swilley
- *Email Marketing in a Digital World: The Basics and Beyond* by Richard C. Hanna, Scott D. Swain and Jason Smith
- *R U #SoLoMo Ready?: Consumers and Brands in the Digital Era* by Stavros Papakonstantinidis, Athanasios Poulis and Prokopis Theodoridis
- *Social Media Marketing: Strategies in Utilizing Consumer-Generated Content* by Emi E. Moriuchi
- *Fostering Brand Community Through Social Media* by William F. Humphrey, Jr., Debra A. Laverie and Shannon B. Rinaldo
- *#Share: How to Mobilize Social Word of Mouth (sWOM)* by Natalie T. Wood and Caroline K. Muñoz
- *The Seven Principles of Digital Business Strategy* by Niall McKeown and Mark Durkin
- *Digital Branding Fever* by Athanasios Poulis, Ioannis Rizomyliotis, and Kleopatra Konstantoulaki

Announcing the Business Expert Press Digital Library

Concise e-books business students need for classroom and research

This book can also be purchased in an e-book collection by your library as

- *a one-time purchase,*
- *that is owned forever,*
- *allows for simultaneous readers,*
- *has no restrictions on printing, and*
- *can be downloaded as PDFs from within the library community.*

Our digital library collections are a great solution to beat the rising cost of textbooks. E-books can be loaded into their course management systems or onto students' e-book readers. The **Business Expert Press** digital libraries are very affordable, with no obligation to buy in future years. For more information, please visit **www.businessexpertpress.com/librarians**. To set up a trial in the United States, please email **sales@businessexpertpress.com**.